T0365292

Cambridge Elements ≡

Elements in Soviet and Post-Soviet History
edited by
Mark Edele
University of Melbourne
Rebecca Friedman
Florida International University

UKRAINIAN LITERATURE

A Wartime Guide for Anglophone Readers

Marko Pavlyshyn
Monash University

CAMBRIDGE
UNIVERSITY PRESS

Shaftesbury Road, Cambridge CB2 8EA, United Kingdom

One Liberty Plaza, 20th Floor, New York, NY 10006, USA

477 Williamstown Road, Port Melbourne, VIC 3207, Australia

314–321, 3rd Floor, Plot 3, Splendor Forum, Jasola District Centre,
New Delhi – 110025, India

103 Penang Road, #05–06/07, Visioncrest Commercial, Singapore 238467

Cambridge University Press is part of Cambridge University Press & Assessment,
a department of the University of Cambridge.

We share the University's mission to contribute to society through the pursuit of
education, learning and research at the highest international levels of excellence.

www.cambridge.org
Information on this title: www.cambridge.org/9781009559072

DOI: 10.1017/9781009559089

First published 2025

A catalogue record for this publication is available from the British Library

ISBN 978-1-009-55907-2 Hardback
ISBN 978-1-009-55906-5 Paperback
ISSN 2753-5290 (online)
ISSN 2753-5282 (print)

For EU product safety concerns, contact us at Calle de José Abascal, 56, 1°, 28003
Madrid, Spain, or email eugpsr@cambridge.org

Ukrainian Literature

A Wartime Guide for Anglophone Readers

Elements in Soviet and Post-Soviet History

DOI: 10.1017/9781009559089
First published online: April 2025

Marko Pavlyshyn
Monash University

Author for correspondence: Marko Pavlyshyn, marko.pavlyshyn@monash.edu

Abstract: *Ukrainian Literature: A Wartime Guide for Anglophone Readers* is an introduction for general readers and students to Ukrainian literature in English translation. It takes as its starting point the responses of Ukrainian poets and prose writers to Russia's full-scale invasion of Ukraine in 2022 and the preceding eight-year war. Each of the Element's ten sections describes a key event in Ukrainian cultural history in its literary context, surveying related works and their authors, Ukrainian and international literary and intellectual movements, and developments in political and social life. The Element gives pre-eminent attention to a theme that the war has foregrounded: the enduringly fraught relationship of Ukraine and Russia. While focussing mainly on texts in Ukrainian, the Element refers to other literary cultures – Polish, Russian, Jewish and Crimean Tatar, among others – whose participants were active on the territory of today's Ukraine.

Keywords: Ukraine, Ukrainian literature, postcolonial literature, war literature, Ukrainian literature in English

ISBNs: 9781009559072 (HB), 9781009559065 (PB), 9781009559089 (OC)
ISSNs: 2753-5290 (online), 2753-5282 (print)

Contents

Foreword

Russia's war against Ukraine, ongoing as I write this, commenced in 2014 and escalated when Russia began its full-scale invasion on 24 February 2022. In discussions and question-and-answer sessions after seminars and other scholarly and semi-scholarly events dedicated to understanding this war, I have often heard members of the audience say that they would be glad to learn about Ukraine through its literature, but cannot because so little of Ukrainian literature is available in English translation.

In fact, a great many English translations of Ukrainian poetry, prose and drama exist, and a surprisingly large number of them are freely available online. But it is true that Ukrainian literature has not been a priority for the most visible English-language publishing houses. It is also true that in order to begin looking for Ukrainian literature in English, potential readers need to know names of authors and titles of works and to have some idea of the content of the latter. It is to such potential readers that *Ukrainian Literature: A Wartime Guide for Anglophone Readers* is addressed.

I assume that these readers are interested in matters that the war has brought to the fore: Ukrainian identity in its present form and at earlier stages of its evolution; Ukraine's relationship with its present aggressor and former colonial master, Russia; and Ukrainians' relationships with other states and ethnocultural groups with which they have historically interacted – Poles, Jews and Crimean Tatars among the latter – on the territory bounded by the present-day internationally recognised border of Ukraine. I also assume that readers are primarily interested in the situation that currently exists and in the past mainly as it helps understand the present. For that reason, the component sections of this Cambridge Element have headings that begin with dates of significant cultural milestones and are arranged in reverse chronological order, proceeding from 2023 to medieval times.

The Element is *a guide for Anglophone readers*. That is to say, first, that its emphasis is on translated texts; of those that are not available in English, I mention only the most important. Second, the Element's purpose being to *guide* the reader, I have tried to make locating the works referred to as straightforward as possible. The following should be noted:

1. If the title of a work appears in the main text in English only, it is the title of the English translation. The two dates that follow in parentheses are the date of original publication (or, in particular instances where this is noted, composition) and the date of publication in English. Where a work was published over a number of years – for example, if it was serialised in a journal – the first and last years of publication are separated by a slash. Only the English translation appears in the list of References.

2. In cases where an untranslated work is mentioned, the title is given, first, in the language of the original in Romanised form. My translation of the title and the year of publication follow in parentheses.

3. Many translations have been published in anthologies, and I often refer to more than one text included in a single such collection. In these instances, the English-language title of the text is followed by the year of its original publication, an abbreviation of the collection's title, and the relevant page numbers. A list of such Abbreviations appears before the list of References at the end of this Element.

4. Some translations, in particular of recent poems and poems by Shevchenko, are most easily found through an online search of the author's name in combination with the title of the work. In such cases, I do not give the year of publication in brackets but state it in the main text if necessary.

5. Many of the books that appear in the list of References, especially older publications, may be downloaded from online repositories. The one that houses the greatest number of books that I refer to is Ukraine-based https://diasporiana.org.ua/, where search terms can be entered in English into the search line (labelled ШУКАТИ). An asterisk at the end of an entry in the list of References or Abbreviations indicates that the text is available through Diasporiana. There also exists an invaluable online bibliography of Ukrainian literary works translated into English (Tarnawsky n.d.).

6. In the main text of this Element, names of persons, places and titles of works are transliterated from the Cyrillic using the Library of Congress Romanisation system modified for ease of reading (initial letters *Є*, *Ю* and *Я* are rendered as *Ye*, *Yu* and *Ya* and terminal *ий* as *y*; the soft sign is transliterated only in the word 'Rus′'). Exceptions are the names of contemporary authors who have published in English; their names are given as they appear in their English-language publications. In the list of References, however, the LC system (without ligatures) is used without modification.

I have called this Element a *wartime* guide not only because it deals with subject matter that the war has made topical but also because in a war there are sides, and this Element sides with Ukraine. It is a partisan text, in solidarity with the sovereign and territorially integral Ukraine whose existence is at present under threat. It is also unapologetically in sympathy with the idea of a Ukrainian nation of individuals of different cultures, languages and faiths, but united by a shared attachment to their state and its democratic civic ideals.

I thank Alessandro Achilli and David Roberts, as well as the anonymous peer reviewers who read drafts of this Element, for their valuable suggestions. I dedicate the Element to its unsung heroes: the translators.

Marko Pavlyshyn
December 2024

2023: Invasion and Defiance

On 1 July 2023, Victoria Amelina, a Ukrainian novelist and poet, died of wounds suffered as a result of a Russian missile strike on Kramatorsk, a city in Eastern Ukraine. Russia began its full-scale invasion of Ukraine on 24 February 2022. The war itself had begun in 2014, soon after the mass civilian protests known as the Euromaidan or the Revolution of Dignity. At that time, Russia occupied Qırım (Crimea) and brought a small part of South-Eastern Ukraine under its control. Eight years of continuous warfare preceded the escalation of 24/2.

Amelina (see Figure 1), born in Lviv in 1986, had a career in information technology management before dedicating herself fully to writing. Born into a Russian-speaking family, she chose to write in Ukrainian. A lyrical poet at first, she made prose her main idiom, returning after the invasion to the brevity

Figure 1 Victoria Amelina, 2018. Photo: Rafał Komorowski. Reproduced unchanged under the Creative Commons Attribution-Share Alike 4.0 International Licence.

and emotional immediacy of poetry. Her debut novel, *Syndrom lystopadu: Homo compatiens* (The Leaf-Fall Syndrome: Homo Compatiens, 2014), was one of the first literary works that incorporated the Euromaidan into its plot. The novel dealt with the ethical person's responsibility to combat injustice: the central character, the 'compassionate human being' of the novel's subtitle, is supernaturally burdened with empathy. He enters into others' consciousness and experiences their sufferings, mentally sharing the pain of the protesters of the Arab Spring in Tunis and Cairo. In the end, he cannot resist joining the Euromaidan protests in Kyiv – not in his mind this time, but in fact. Amelina's second and only other published novel, *Dim dlia Doma* (A Home for Dom, 2017), is whimsically framed as a first-person narrative told by a poodle named Dom. A sympathetic portrayal of urban life in the last years of the USSR and at the start of Ukraine's independence, it tells of a family, once part of the old Soviet military elite, whose members must modify their loyalties and identities in a new Ukraine where they no longer enjoy privilege.

Amelina's wartime poems, in keeping with much Ukrainian poetry written in the wake of the invasion, formulated a new and starkly polarised world view, loyal to compatriots and outraged by Russia, the atrocities perpetrated by its army, and its history of colonialism: 'You're brothers, perhaps? / No, our arms crossed / not in embrace, but in battle / ... As our battle begins / You'd do well not to ask / Why we resemble those / who have killed us since time began' (Amelina 2022).

Victoria Amelina's return to poetry was part of a broad cultural phenomenon: the burgeoning of poetic creativity in response to the war. From at least the time of Taras Shevchenko (1814–61), celebrated as Ukraine's national poet, poetry helped define and defend Ukrainian national identity in the face of colonial predation. After 2014, poets – many with established reputations, but also a great number of amateurs – eagerly embraced this task. An anthology of contemporary lyrical poetry about the war published in 2022 included works by no fewer than 142 authors (Sydorzhevs'kyi 2022). Poetry is well suited to recording personal responses to war: lyrical poems, traditionally brief, take less time to compose than works of other genres; their task is to express emotions; and the boundary between the 'speaker' of the poem and the poet as a real person is often blurred. Social media has made possible the presentation of poetry to the public without the mediation of publishers. The poetry of amateurs may well be less sophisticated than that of established poets, but both record and reflect on the feelings of men and women in their wartime roles as soldiers, volunteers, providers of essential services, refugees or carers. Both reflect on same large themes: the preciousness and fragility of life; the meaning of suffering and self-sacrifice; and the individual's obligation to the community.

While anthologies of war poetry have proliferated in Ukraine, they have appeared in translation as well. Among the collections available in English are Oksana Maksymchuk's and Max Rosochinsky's *Words for War* (2017), Anatoly Kudryavitsky's *The Frontier* (2017), Kalpana Singh-Chitnis's *Sunflowers* (2022) and Carolyn Forché's and Ilya Kaminsky's *In the Hour of War* (2023). Translations favour the work of established poets over the verse of poetic newcomers, but in wartime Ukraine, straightforwardness and sincerity are embraced as poetic virtues, while 'professional', 'literary' expression seems extravagant – alongside ambiguity, ornament, playfulness and other residues of the postmodernism of the 1990s and 2000s. As Halyna Kruk (b. 1974), herself a literary scholar, put it in the opening poem of her provocatively named collection, *Crash Course in Molotov Cocktails*, 'the main thing is not to forget that none of this was about literature' (Kruk 2023: 31; see also Kruk 2024).

Among the topics that contemporary Ukrainian poetry *is* about are the emotions that the war evokes: fear, such as a mother's fear for her children in Kruk's 'In a Dream'; anger, like that of the lyrical subject at being separated from her family in 'How I Killed' by Lyuba Yakimchuk (b. 1985), a native of Donbas and author of the collection *Apricots of Donbas* (2015, 2021); and grief, such as the anguish caused by the ruination of people, their homes and cities that Marianna Kiyanovska (b. 1973), who had explored historical trauma in *Voices of Babyn Yar* (2017, 2022), brings to expression in 'the heart trapped in guilt-pain'. On the other hand, there is love: love as the sensation that suffuses soldiers as they go about their dangerous duties, as in 'The First Letter to the Corinthians' by Artur Dron (b. 2000); love for home, depicted by Ostap Slyvynsky (b. 1978) in 'Latifa' as most keenly felt when that home is lost; love for one's comrades-in-arms and one's family; and even love for one's fellow creatures, exemplified in 'Let me tell you a story', Maksym Kryvtsov's poignant portrait of the cat that is his companion in the trenches. Kryvtsov (1990–2024) was killed at the front shortly after the publication of his first collection of poems.

The war challenges its lyrical chroniclers to document thoughts and feelings at moments of trauma or catastrophe. In his laconic 'Debaltseve Prayer', Volodymyr Tymchuk (b. 1979) transforms the soldier's certainty that he faces insuperable odds into a mental prayer for the dead and a plea to be given the chance to improve the world. Natalka Marynchak (b. 1981) relates images of the carnage after the bursting of a shell to the colours of Ukrainian embroidery ('our embroideries are like notches red on the bare flesh ...'), while the Russian-language Ukrainian poet Lyudmyla Khersonska (b. 1964) observes that 'Buried in a human neck, a bullet looks like an eye, sewn in' (Khersonska 2023: 15). In 'Caterpillar', Lyuba Yakimchuk terrifyingly reconstructs the dissociated pictures that arise in a woman's mind before and while she suffers serial rape. The agony of a veteran who lives with ineradicable memories, and the agony of the spouse who cares for and suffers with him, is the theme of 'April 6' by Kateryna Kalytko (b. 1982), author of the collection *Nobody Knows Us Here and We Don't Know Anyone* (2019, 2022).

Serhiy Zhadan's strategies for making the war tangible include depicting its impact on people at the margins of society: the tattoo artist who has become politicised ('Needle'), the alcoholic who is also an esoteric poet ('Headphones') or the Seventh-Day Adventist ('Sect'). Zhadan (b. 1974; see Figure 2), a poet, novelist, singer and political activist, remained in Kharkiv as a volunteer when the city came under bombardment and in June 2024 enlisted in the army. His collection *How Fire Descends* begins with poems written in 2021 and 2022; in contrast to the hard-bitten irony of much of his earlier poetry, some of these 'New Poems' soften the pain of war with hopes for a newly meaningful life and a return to lost homes.

Few contemporary Ukrainian poets reject war absolutely, independent of the justice of the cause for which it is fought. Yuri Izdryk (b. 1962), whose nonconformist cultural activities brought him fame and notoriety in the 1990s, is one of the rare exceptions, deeming war, including 'this war', 'a chance not to kill anyone' ('Make Love'). More characteristic is the stoic stance of poets who acknowledge war's hellishness, but concede the absence of alternatives to fighting it – Iryna Shuvalova (b. 1986) in 'Volunteer', or Borys

Figure 2 Serhiy Zhadan, 2020. Photo: Venzz. Reproduced unchanged under the Creative Commons Attribution-Share Alike 4.0 International Licence.

Humenyuk (b. 1965), who volunteered in 2014 and has been missing in action since late 2022. Humenyuk likens a soldier who keeps his rifle in good order to a father swaddling his infant, while a trench becomes a symbolic place of encounter with earth, land and country, all three captured by the single Ukrainian word *zemlia* ('When You Clean Your Weapon').

The pathos of much Ukrainian war poetry is that of endurance and resistance, which Natalka Marynchak captures in her image of a heart of reinforced concrete ('and each of us will have a separate war'). 'We Won't Go Anywhere!' declares Oleksandr Kozynets (b. 1988). In 'Abraham is walking', Boris Khersonsky recalls that Christ died and arose again through His own power, implying that Ukraine's life force is a similarly self-generated. Such invocations of Biblical narrative are not uncommon in Ukrainian war poetry: Halyna Kruk's 'and Jesus ascended' draws an analogy between Christ's cruci-fixion and the atrocities committed in Bucha (Kruk 2023: 35).

Many poets invoke the motif of the inadequacy of language in the face of the brutality of war. For Marianna Savka (b. 1973), poetry in wartime is a hot-air balloon that has turned to lead ('We wrote poems …'). Ella Yevtushenko (b. 1996) laments the failure of words to convey the horrors of occupation ('#BuchaMassacre'). In Lyuba Yakimchuk's 'Decomposition', the fragmenta-tion of the names of cities mirrors the destruction of the cities themselves: 'hansk' is what remains of Luhansk, and Debaltseve breaks up into 'deb', 'alt' and 'eve'. Iryna Shuvalova, author of the collection *Pray to the Empty Wells*, doubts the morality of writing poetry amid war-inflicted suffering ('the unspeakable'). But poetic language can also be a weapon. Yulia Musakovska (b. 1982), who in 'The God of Submission' mocks non-resistance to violence and acceptance of victimhood (Musakovska 2024: 102), asserts that 'There is nothing more durable, / nothing less fleeting' than 'Our words, hard and swollen with rage, / black from grief, / like the concrete covering of an old bomb shelter' ('Words'). For Zhadan, 'it turns out that the language is mightier than the fear of speaking' ('Perhaps It's Time to Start Now'). Kateryna Kalytko's poem 'Here, take this language, woman' instructs its reader, 'Use it [language] to shoot. … There are plenty of bullets, don't spare them, / if they run out – / make new ones out of words'.

The relationship between language and national identity has been a motif of Ukrainian literature, intellectual debate and politics since the nineteenth cen-tury. Many Ukrainian writers and poets were born in parts of Ukraine where the Russian language prevailed over Ukrainian in daily use. In independent Ukraine, some writers, while identifying as Ukrainians, wrote in Russian. Outrage at the Russian invasion made it difficult for some to continue doing so. Boris Khersonsky, who previously had written in Russian only, began writing in Ukrainian as well. Others, such as Iya Kiva (b. 1984), abandoned Russian altogether. For twenty-five years, Volodymyr Rafeyenko (b. 1969), a native of Donetsk, had written and published in Russian. He fled his native city in 2014 and settled near Bucha, intending at first to alternate writing novels in Ukrainian and Russian. But after the atrocities of which Bucha became a symbol, he wrote, 'never again in my life would I write or publish any of my work in Russian. I no longer want anything to do with a culture of murderers and rapists' ('I Once Wrote – and Spoke, and Thought – in Russian … No More'). Rafeyenko's last novel in Russian (a Ukrainian translation by Marianna Kiyanovska appeared simultaneously), *The Length of Days* (2017, 2023), was a phantasmagoria in the gothic manner in which the grotesque is the appropriate mode for representing life in the city of Z, a transparent allegory of Donetsk. *Mondegreen* (Rafeyenko 2019, 2022), Rafeyenko's first novel in Ukrainian, also an exemplar of non-realistic prose, depicts the tribulations of a newcomer to Kyiv and to the Ukrainian language, a refugee from his place and culture of origin.

Many authors found intolerable what they diagnosed as the complicity of Russian culture in Russian imperialism and its most recent embodiment, the invasion of Ukraine. Equally offensive for them was the failure of many in the West, including fellow intellectuals, to condemn the colonial criminality of the Russian state or the widespread acceptance by Russian society of Russia's war aims. Oksana Zabuzhko (b. 1960), a poet, writer, philosopher and one of the pre-eminent voices of Ukrainian feminism from the late 1980s onward, writing in the *Times Literary Supplement*, berated the West for its blindness to Russia's totalitarianism and long history of crimes against humanity. The West's endeavours to grasp the rationality of evil, Zabuzhko contends, glide easily into acceptance of its normality; hence the failure to comprehend the pathological otherness of Russia, of which Russian literature, deeply admired by the West, is a direct expression: 'Russian literature has, for 200 years, painted a picture of the world in which the criminal is to be pitied, not condemned. We should sympathize with him, for "there are no guilty people in the world" (Tolstoy)' (Zabuzhko 2022: 7). In a similar vein, Donetsk-born Olena Stiazhkina (b. 1968) in her 'War Diary' reflected on the 'little man' in Russian literature who is unable to resist the compulsions that drive him to crime. As an example of such ethical paralysis, Stiazhkina holds up the character of Gerasim in Ivan Turgenev's short story 'Mumu' (1852), a text taught as a literary classic in Soviet schools. Gerasim drowns the dog he loves because, to his mind, his circumstances leave him no alternative (*U22*: 22). Turgenev's story also figures in Zabuzhko's 'No Guilty People' and in 'The Ouroboros Path', an essay in which the writer and film director Iryna Tsilyk (b. 1982) decries the instincts that manifest themselves in the outrages of the invasion and the historical tradition to which they belong: 'primitive desire to humiliate another human being, to destroy, to desecrate someone else's body and spirit, to close someone's mouth, to tear tender flesh roughly, to "punish" someone else, their dignity, their otherness, their right to say no' (*U22*: 157).

Anger is the dominant tone of Ukrainian writers' essayistic responses to the war. But just as some war poetry is about love, so, too, is a strand of reflective prose. In 'To You, Beloved River', Taras Prokhasko (b. 1968) records the experience of loving one's country as a sensation that moves body and mind: 'Landscape comprises something seen by the brain of the heart and the heart of the brain . . . . To be able to be yourself in your landscape is to be in harmony with your inner and outer world' (*U22*: 64). Even in war, there is space for the idyll.

One of the genres to which Ukrainian authors have turned during the war is the diary, in which the recording of events of the traumatic present is often accompanied by commentary, interpretation and digression into general reflection. Such are Rafeyenko's narratives of his family's flight from the vicinity of Bucha (*U22*: 57–62, 73–8, 83–8), Olena Stiazhkina's *Ukraine, War, Love: A Donetsk Diary* (2024) about events between March and August 2014, Zhadan's *Sky Above Kharkiv* (2023b) and *Diary of an Invasion* (2022) by Andrey Kurkov (b. 1961), a prolific novelist and perhaps Ukraine's most translated contemporary author. Kurkov writes in Russian but makes a point of identifying himself as a Ukrainian writer. He had used the same genre in his account of the Euromaidan protests, *Ukrainian Diaries: Dispatches from Kiev [Kyiv]* (2014).

Since 2014, many Ukrainian authors have felt the need to respond to the war with prose that is compelling and aesthetically charged, but at the same time truthful, even documentary. Witnessing is one of the tasks addressed by Olesya Khromeychuk (b. 1983) in *The Death of a Soldier Told by his Sister* (2022), a memoir originally written in English; another, as the author puts it in her preface, is 'to use the privilege that living in Western Europe gave me to remind the world that our [i.e., the West's] freedom is just as fragile as that of our fellow Europeans in Ukraine' (Khromeychuk 2022: 9). The memoir records the author's efforts to supply a soldier in a distant country with what he needs (good boots, for example); her shock on discovering, through Facebook, that her brother has been killed; her incapacity to talk about his death; the nightmare of arranging the funeral; the renewed relevance of her brother's death after 24/2; and the enduring experience of loss and survivor guilt.

Like *Stories from the Trenches* (2020, 2024) by Dmytro Stepanenko (b. 1975), *Absolute Zero* (2016, 2020) by Artem Chekh (pseudonym of Artem Cherednyk, b. 1985) is an example of what has come to be called 'combatants' prose': war-themed writing by soldiers or veterans of the war. Chekh first served in the army in 2015–16. He returned to the front after 24/2 and sustained a contusion near Bakhmut where fighting was protracted and especially fierce. *Absolute Zero* is a series of short essays, chronologically arranged, which provide snapshots of army life from recruitment to demobilisation. The book's central theme is the mundaneness of military life, characterised by drudgery and discomfort even more than by danger. Military assignments appear illogical, well-meaning volunteers wrongheaded, differences of class and education difficult to overcome. But the friendships that develop among soldiers have depth and warmth. There is no heroism, only the conviction that there is no alternative to doing what one must do. *Absolute Zero* is autobiographical; Chekh's later novels, *Raion "D"* (District D, 2019) and *Khto ty takyi* (Who Are You? 2021), set mainly in his home city, Cherkasy, are partly so.

Many novels written before 24/2 reflected on war-related problems – trauma, guilt, identity and civic responsibility – whether the war was their central theme or not. Many adopted even-handed stances toward the warring sides, even as they portrayed the occupation and its minions in negative colours. The contrast between two novels illustrates the range of attitudes toward the war in pre-24/2 fiction. *Daughter* (2019, 2023), the debut novel of Tamara Horikha Zernia (pseudonym of Tamara Duda, b. 1976), is set in Donbas after 2014. It is the story of a young woman who, after witnessing violence against supporters of the Euromaidan and the barbarity of the occupiers, supports Ukrainian soldiers as a volunteer. *Za spynoiu* (Behind One's Back, 2019) by Haska Shyyan (b. 1980) also has a woman as the novel's central character. For this first-person narrator, however, the war is a challenge to the life of choices and opportunities that she enjoys as a member of the country's young professional elite – privileges she is not inclined to forgo.

Between his diaries of the Euromaidan and the full-scale invasion, Andrey Kurkov wrote the novel *Grey Bees* (2018, 2020). The narrative of a beekeeper's journey from his home in the 'grey zone' (the no-man's land between the front lines in Donbas) to Qırım and back underscores the author's sympathy with Crimean Tatars and condemns their plight under occupation. Of Kurkov's many novels *Death and the Penguin* (1996, 2001), the first to be translated into English, is still the best known. Kurkov's works, in which crime fiction often joins with elements of mystery, are characterised by identifiably Ukrainian settings and ingenious, at times eccentric, plots.

Serhiy Zhadan's *The Orphanage* (2017, 2021), a novel set in the war zone in Donbas, reflects on the morality of not taking sides. The novel goes to some lengths not to specify the allegiance of the combatants represented, nor the sources of the shelling that terrifies the civilian population. The central character, Pasha, a teacher of Ukrainian despite the Russian name by which he is generally known, endeavours to avoid involvement in the war, but cannot help confronting it as he brings his nephew home across disputed territory. His journey across the treacherous terrain teaches him that neutrality is neither psychologically nor ethically sustainable.

Zhadan, the author of numerous collections of poetry – *A New Orthography* (2020) and *How Fire Descends* (Zhadan 2023a) are available in English – has done much in his novels to create a literary portrait of urban, post-industrial Eastern Ukraine. *Depeche Mode* (2004, 2013), *Voroshilovgrad* (2010, 2016) and *Mesopotamia* (2014, 2018) depict a tough, often criminal low-life environment that is home to characters who are male, young, insecure, violent, given to the use of alcohol and other drugs, and profane in their language. Zhadan's characteristic flat, ironic style and dark humour are well represented in his often anthologised story, 'Owner of the Best Gay Bar' (2006, *WCD*: 181–218).

In no contemporary Ukrainian novel do the difficult questions raised by the war receive more serious attention than in *Amadoka* (2020), a vast, more than 900-page novel by Sophia Andrukhovych (b. 1982). Sophia Andrukhovych's earlier novels differed greatly from each other, and from *Amadoka*, in content and form. *Somha* (Salmon 2007) was a first-person narrative marked by a degree of openness about female sexuality still relatively unusual in Ukrainian literature, while *Felix Austria* (Andrukhovych, S. 2014, 2024) was a work of gothic suspense superimposed over a lovingly detailed representation of middle-class life in a small multi-ethnic town in Austria-Hungary.

In the frame narrative of *Amadoka*, a woman, Romana (the Ukrainian word for novel is *roman*), claims to recognise a veteran of the war, afflicted with amnesia and disfigured beyond recognition, as her husband. Romana purports to reactivate his memory and restore his knowledge of who he is – but in fact tries to impose a new identity on him. The plot compels readers to ask: how does physical and mental trauma impinge on consciousness of the self? What is memory, and what ethical issues arise in the process of its transmission? These queries, as well as complex and inconclusive answers to them, echo through subplots that cover many painful periods of Ukraine's twentieth-century history. The love story of Pinkhas and Uliana unfolds against the background of the Second World War and the Holocaust. Their romance involves a quest for Amadoka, a lake that appears on ancient maps but whose reality is as questionable as that of all the novel's narratives. Replete with arcane knowledge, *Amadoka* confronts readers with such figures from the history of the Ukrainian lands as the Baroque sculptor Johann Georg Pinsel, the eighteenth-century mystic Hryhorii Skovoroda, the founder of Hassidism Baal Shem Tov and, at greatest length, the novelist, literary scholar and Soviet spy Viktor

Petrov. A tour de force of a novel, Amadoka is a probe into the open or only partly healed wounds of the history of Europe.

1992: Independence Established, Enjoyed and Explored

In January 1992, a short novel titled *Recreations* (1992, 1998) by Yuri Andrukhovych, a poet with an established reputation for iconoclasm, opened the first issue of *Suchasnist* (The Present) to appear in Ukraine. Since 1961, the periodical had been published by émigré Ukrainians in Munich and New York. Emphatically anti-Soviet, it advocated for Ukraine's political independence and championed modern tendencies in Ukrainian literature. The journal's move took place at a momentous time in Ukraine's history. Efforts by Mikhail Gorbachev, the leader of the Communist Party of the USSR since 1985, to reenergise the Soviet Union by liberalising its authoritarian political system led to an attempted coup d'état by forces nostalgic for the old dictatorial state of affairs. The coup failed; in its aftermath, on 24 August 1991, the Ukrainian parliament proclaimed Ukraine's independence, an act endorsed by more than 90 per cent of Ukraine's voters in a referendum held on 1 December 1991.

Recreations, published immediately after these events, was simultaneously an expression of the profound breach with the Soviet past that the declaration of independence represented, and a provocative refusal to endorse unconditionally the discourse of national patriotism that had gained momentum in the years preceding independence. The novel told the story of young Ukrainian poets attending an adrenalin-charged carnival, full of patriotic fervour and erotic energy, much like the Chervona Ruta (Red Rue Flower) Festival in Chernivtsi in 1989. *Recreations* caused a minor scandal by debunking one of the most cherished Ukrainian national myths: that of the dignity of the poet and the poet's sacral role in embodying and regenerating the nation. The novel was ironic and sceptical toward staunch ideological positions and unitary 'grand narratives', whether of the construction of a communist paradise or of liberation to create a utopian nation state, giving critics cause to associate it with Western postmodernism. Indeed, *Recreations* revelled in postmodern formal devices, playfully mixing stylistic registers and juxtaposing unrelated things in long and comically eccentric lists.

Recreations also made a geopolitical statement: it expressed nostalgia for the Austro-Hungarian Empire, of which the Western part of Ukraine where Andrukhovych was born had been part. Later, in text after text, and especially in his resonant essays (see Andrukhovych, 2018a) and his public addresses (see Figure 3), Andrukhovych underscored the participation of his homeland in the landscape and culture of Europe and decried its colonially imposed and

Figure 3 Yuri Andrukhovych addresses the Euromaidan, Kyiv, December 2013. Photo: A1. Reproduced under the Creative Commons CC0 1.0 Universal Public Domain Dedication.

unnatural connection to Russia. The alienness of Russia was the theme of his satirical novel *The Moscoviad* (1993, 2008) with its phantasmagorical depiction of the imperial capital. But Andrukhovych did not unconditionally embrace Europe or the West: resentment against their condescension toward, and lack of interest in, Ukraine was a central theme of *Perverzion* (1996, 2005), Andrukhovych's satirical representation of a Western scholarly conference, and *Twelve Circles* (2003, 2015). *Twelve Circles*, which achieved a degree of notoriety for its masculinist reinvention of the biography of the subdued and introspective poet Bohdan Ihor Antonych (1909–37), depicted the contemporary human mind as yearning for stable, reassuring certainties while melancholically aware that they are unattainable.

Andrukhovych began his literary career as a poet; two anthologies of his poetry are available in English (Andrukhovych, Y. 2018b; 2024). The second half of the 1980s saw a fashion in Ukrainian literature for eccentrically titled poetic groups: Luhosad (the name comprised fragments of the members' surnames), Propala hramota (Lost Certificate) and Nova deheneratsiia (New Degeneration), among others. In 1985, together with fellow poets Oleksandr Irvanets and Viktor Neborak, Andrukhovych formed the most celebrated such team: Bu-Ba-Bu. Bu-Ba-Bu's carnivalesque essence was captured in the words whose initial syllables made up its title: *burlesk* (burlesque), *balahan* (a temporary structure for circus or theatre shows) and *bufonada* (buffoonery). Bu-Ba-Bu combined poetry with theatrical and musical performance and, above all, offense to conventional taste, most notoriously in the 'poeso-opera' *Chrysler Imperial*, staged in the Lviv opera house in 1992. Andrukhovych's poems of the period were characterised by mystery, gothic sensationalism, verbal fireworks and, in such poems as 'Jamaica the Cossack' and 'India', a paradoxical mixing of the local and the exotic. Bu-Ba-Bu's penchant for provocation was exemplified in Irvanets's 'Love', where exhortations to love Oklahoma, Indiana and a string of other states of the USA parodied Volodymyr Sosiura's patriotic poem 'Love Ukraine' (1944). Neborak's poem cycle 'The Flying Head' echoed the experimentation of the Ukrainian avant-garde of the 1920s (Neborak 2005). The transformative zest of the times also found expression in the work of Petro Midianka, Yurko Pozaiak, Atilla Mohylny, Kostiantyn Moskalets, Ivan Luchuk and Nazar Honchar, small selections of whose poems appear in the bilingual anthology *A Hundred Years of Youth* (*100Y*), and in the poems of Volodymyr Tsybulko collected in *An Eye in the Belfry* (2005).

In the 1990s, the city of Ivano-Frankivsk, previously called Stanislav, became the focal point of much innovative literary activity. The 'Stanislav Phenomenon' encompassed writers born in 1960 or later. One of them, Volodymyr Yeshkiliev (b. 1965), wittily classified contemporary Ukrainian literary discourse under three categories: PM (postmodern), NM (neomodern) and TR (traditional and rustic). The writers discussed hitherto in this section fell within the orbit of 'PM discourse', as did Yeshkiliev himself and two of the Stanislav Phenomenon's most original writers: Yuri Izdryk and Taras Prokhasko. Izdryk, a poet, prose writer, composer, musician, visual artist and performance artist, edited the journal *Chetver* (Thursday), whose texts and illustrations reflected the self-referential and ironic, yet philosophically challenging and erudite, qualities characteristic of postmodernism. Only the first of his short novels is available in English. *Wozzeck* (1997, 2006), like Alban Berg's atonal opera of that name (1925), articulates the tragedy of a human being thrust into an irrational and hostile world. 'Necropolis' (1998, 1999), a text by Taras Prokhasko that might well have been written to illustrate the ambiguity and structural quirkiness of 'PM discourse', is the story of a character writing a novel and reflecting on the philosophical questions raised by doing so. Philosophical discussion with St Augustine, Heidegger and Husserl is at the heart of Prokhasko's surreal 'Essai de déconstruction' (1998, 2022). Transgenerational and incestuous love figures in the mythological world of his novel *The UnSimple* (2002, 2007/2011).

A different form of resistance to Soviet traditionalism characterised the austere prose of Viacheslav Medvid (b. 1951), Yevhen Pashkovsky (b. 1965) and Oles Ulianenko (1962–2010). Pashkovsky's pathos of solidarity with suffering humanity and his depictions of the historical torments endured by his people demand for their expression a syntax that resists easy reading. The short story 'Five Loaves and Two Fishes' (1994, *FTW*: 89–97) exemplifies this conjuncture of ethical stance and prose style, a constant of Pashkovsky's longer, untranslated, works. Ulianenko, whose biography included episodes of stark material hardship, created prose as intense in its representation of psychological anguish and social misery as Pashkovsky's. Ulianenko focussed on people surviving on the peripheries of society: in *Stalinka* (1994, 2021), the first of his fourteen novels, the narrative of an escapee from a mental asylum intertwines with that of the leader of a criminal youth gang.

The rebellion against Soviet ideological and aesthetic orthodoxies immediately before and after the renewal of Ukraine's independence had its (admittedly slender) roots in the 1970s and 1980s. In theory, Soviet artists were obliged to abide by the precepts of Socialist Realism, which meant advocating for the goals of social transformation as interpreted by the Communist Party. Works of art were therefore to be accessible to the average Soviet citizen; intellectual complexity or 'excessive' focus on artistic form was to be avoided. In practice, however, by the 1980s, deviations from these prescriptions could be tolerated, provided that works did not directly challenge Party ideology or the primacy of the 'elder brother', Russia, among the nationalities of the USSR. Non-traditional works that the state appeared to tolerate included those that blurred the boundary between realism and fantasy in the spirit of Latin American magic realism. In Ukraine, such 'chimerical novels', whose early examples included *The Swan Flock* (1971, 1982) and *Green Mills* (1977, 1984) by Vasyl Zemlyak (1923–77), provided a platform from which the novelist Valeriy Shevchuk (b. 1939) could launch his subtle campaign to make the Ukrainian reading public aware of the historical depth and alluring complexity of Ukrainian culture.

Shevchuk began his writing career in the 1960s as one of several young authors whose prose offered unideological, often idyllic, representations of the everyday life of ordinary people. Then, for a decade, his works were banned from publication. When his books began appearing again, they included the novel *Dim na hori* (The House on the Hill, 1983), in the first part of which supernatural events infiltrate the initially realistic narrative of a veteran's return from the war in 1946. The second part, published in English as an independent work titled *Breath of Evil* (Shevchuk 2016), comprises fourteen tensely plotted narratives set in a premodern, vaguely seventeenth-century Ukrainian Cossack society characterised by a complex interplay of folklore, superstition and religious belief. Translators have warmed to this gothic side of Shevchuk's oeuvre, other examples of which are *Eye of the Abyss* (1996, 2004/2007) and *Lunar*

Pain (1984, 2010). Shevchuk treats the stuff of history in a more rationalist manner in *The Meek Shall Inherit* (1983, 1989), a novel that satirically retells the lives of monks that were piously recorded in the thirteenth-century *Pateryk of the Kyivan Caves Monastery*. The greater part of Shevchuk's fictional work, however, is dedicated to narratives of the ordinary-yet-extraordinary folk in small Ukrainian cities, especially his home town of Zhytomyr, as in the case of his long short story 'The Moon's Cuckoo from the Swallow's Nest' (1992, *FTW*: 99–136). Culturally as significant as Shevchuk's reclamation of the medieval and early modern periods for Ukrainian fiction were his editions in modern Ukrainian of literary texts from those periods: they challenged, if only by implication, the Russocentricity of the official version of history cultivated in the USSR.

A more explicit and politically consequential challenge to the Soviet belief system came as Ukrainian writers responded to the Chornobyl disaster. The negligence leading to the fire, explosions and uncontrolled release of radiation at the Chornobyl nuclear power plant in April 1986; the deaths of first responders; the irradiation of local residents and, above all, Soviet authorities' reluctance to inform the public of the situation undermined social trust in the Soviet regime. The ecological movement became the earliest form of tolerated civil society activism in the USSR. Journalists and writers who reported on the Chornobyl disaster garnered considerable public authority. Iurii Shcherbak, the medical researcher and writer who authored *Chernobyl [Chornobyl]: A Documentary Story* (1987, 1989), became independent Ukraine's first minister for the environment and, later, ambassador to the United States. *The Chornobyl Madonna* (1987, 2016) by Volodymyr Yavorivsky (1942–2021), based on the author's interviews with affected people, took *hlasnist* (Russian *glasnost*), openness, the slogan of Gorbachev's liberalisation agenda, at face value. It criticised not merely the failures of the regime's response to Chornobyl, but the distempers of Soviet society in general. Yavorivsky became one of the leading figures of the oppositional National Movement of Ukraine (known as Rukh), joining his colleagues, the poets Dmytro Pavlychko and Ivan Drach, author of a long poem on Chornobyl. All three served as members of parliament in Ukraine on the eve of independence and afterwards.

As the 1980s drew to a close, writers murdered by the regime in the 1930s and unmentionable thereafter were rehabilitated and their writings published. Crimes of the Soviet regime were openly discussed. Previously prohibited dramatic works and patriotic songs were performed in public. These events in the literary and cultural sphere marked the transformation in Ukraine of the movement to reform the Soviet system into a movement for national rebirth and, ultimately, independence.

The insurrection against Socialist Realism by Andrukhovych and other cultural provocateurs was part of this process. Other poets who had been active for some time, but were in official disfavour, now received attention. Some had rejected traditional forms in favour of free verse, or had created complex, even hermetic works that placed intellectual demands on their readers. All had turned away from Soviet-style poetry of ideological statement. Oleh Lysheha (1949–2014), banned between 1971 and 1988 and known, in addition to his poetry, for the extreme asceticism of his lifestyle, created poetry influenced by American modernism and the philosophical and poetic cultures of Asia. His *Selected Poems* (1999) and the collection *Dream Bridge* (2022) are available in English; individual examples of his numbered 'Songs' appear on many web pages. Hryhorii (Hrytsko) Chubai (1949–1982), a focal personality of the Lviv cultural underground of the late 1960s and 1970s, wrote allusive, image-rich free verse with mystical overtones. His poetry, unpublished until the 1990s, is represented in English by 'The Search for the Accomplice' (*100Y*: 510–27) and a selection in *WCD* (31–41).

The 'Kyiv School' of poets, formed as early as 1969, included Mykola Vorobiov (b. 1941), Vasyl Holoborodko (b. 1945) and Viktor Kordun (1946–2005). *Mountain and Flower* (2020) is a selection in English of Vorobiov's deceptively simple, sometimes laconic, mainly first-person lyrical poems. A delicate, almost Romantic, sacralising evocation of nature characterises Holoborodko's 'Night Song' and 'On the Corner of that Street' (*100Y*: 469, 471) as much as Kordun's 'Psalm of Loneliness' and 'Psalm of White Silk' (*100Y*: 475, 477).

One of the best-known Ukrainian poetic texts of the late 1980s was 'We'll Not Die in Paris' by Natalka Bilotserkivets (b. 1954). Like her 'Picasso Elegy' (*FTW*: 155), the poem expressed a yearning to experience the culture of contemporary Europe. Two collections of Bilotserkivets's poetry have appeared in English: *Eccentric Days of Hope and Sorrow* (2021) and *Subterranean Fire* (2022). Other notable poets of the period are represented by small assortments in English-language anthologies: Liudmyla Taran, Vasyl Herasymiuk, Ihor Rymaruk (in *100Y*) and Ivan Malkovych (in *WCD*).

In the domain of prose, Volodymyr Dibrova (b. 1951) offered satirical reflections on Soviet reality, their humour sometimes nostalgic and gentle, as in *Beatles Songs* (1991, excerpted in *FTW*: 24–30), and sometimes, when the object of attack was Soviet authoritarianism, sharp and grotesque, as in *Peltse* (1991, 1996). Yuri Vynnychuk (b. 1952), some of whose tales were collected in *The Windows of Time Frozen* (2000), combines fine narrative craftsmanship in the tradition of magic realism with black humour and an eroticism that borders dangerously on pornography and misogyny. His prose emphasises the cultural and linguistic specificity of Western Ukraine, whether contemporary or, as in his novel *Tango of Death* (2012, 2019), historical. The gothic is the metier of Halyna Pahutiak's uncanny tales and of Vasyl Gabor's *Book of Exotic Dreams and Real Events* (1999, 2023).

The rise of feminism in intellectual and literary circles was perhaps the most momentous cultural development in Ukraine in the period immediately after 1991. At its centre was Oksana Zabuzhko (see Figure 4). In Zabuzhko's collections *A Kingdom of Fallen Statues* (1996) and *Selected Poems* (2020), politics is often inseparable from eros. Both anthologies commence with 'Clytemnestra', in which a strong woman's vengeance against her violent and treacherous husband and king is an allegory of rebellion against the patriarchal order. Zabuzhko's provocatively titled *Fieldwork in Ukrainian Sex* (1996, 2011) became one of the most widely read Ukrainian books of the decade. The central character, Oksana, is a dauntingly intelligent, agonisingly self-critical woman poet on a fellowship in

Figure 4 Oksana Zabuzhko, 2008. Photo: Marko Pavlyshyn.

the United States. In a cascade of breathless sentences, she probes the physiology and psychology of her erotic passion, which is also political: the magnetism between Oksana and her lover is intensified by their both being staunch Ukrainians alert to their country's history and the injustices that its people have endured. This consciousness of grievance puts them at odds with both the post-Soviet world and the West: in both milieus, Russocentric perspectives remain in force. Zabuzhko revisited the issue of Soviet colonialism in the much longer, but stylistically similar, novel *Museum of Abandoned Secrets* (2009, 2012), a family saga spanning three generations between the Second World War and the 2000s. Zabuzhko's finely structured story 'Girls' (1999, *Herstories*: 181–202) explores the friendship of two adolescent girls, which reveals itself as a homoerotic passion and ends with their mutual betrayals.

Eugenia Kononenko (b. 1959) is the author of short stories and novels about women's social and psychological problems in a post-Soviet environment: changing workplace and domestic roles, the need to work abroad and the complications accompanying marriage with men from rich countries. A recurrent theme is the predicament of highly educated Ukrainian women offended by Western condescension toward people from formerly Soviet countries (see, e.g., 'It Just Didn't Work Out', *Herstories*: 148–54). Kononenko's short novel *A Russian Story* (2012, 2013) tells of a Kyiv intellectual, a man whose story is 'Russian' because his life with its compromises and failures, including his marriage of convenience to a Russophile American literary scholar, are consequences of the geopolitical fact that Ukraine was one of the subordinate parts of the USSR.

Maria Matios (b. 1959) is a prolific and popular writer who has twice been elected to the Ukrainian parliament. Many of her novels are set in Bukovyna, a region of Ukraine that borders Romania. Her works cover the periods of Bukovyna's incorporation into Austria-Hungary, Romania, the USSR and independent Ukraine. Wars and border changes, the Ukrainian Insurgent Army, the atrocities of the Soviet occupation and the often conflictual interaction of ethnicities – Ukrainians, Jews, Romanians and Russians – form the background to Matios's stories of the lives of ordinary people. Matios's *Sweet Darusya* (2002/2003, 2019), *Hardly Ever Otherwise* (2007, 2010) and *The Russky Woman* (2008, 2011) are novels replete with unexpected plot turns, supernatural events, erotic passions and depictions of violence, especially of men against women.

Works of fiction by Ukrainian women writers that appeared in the 2000s and were translated into English include *Episodic Memory* (2007, 2015) by Liubov Holota (b. 1949), a tale set in a village in the 1970s where members of different generations cultivate different memories of the past, and *Forgottenness* (2016, 2024) by Tanja Maljartschuk (b. 1983), who writes in Ukrainian and German.

Forgottenness interweaves the stories of a present-day researcher and the Ukrainian political theorist Viacheslav Lypynsky (1882–1931). Some novels by women explore contemporary Ukrainian life while entertaining their readers with intriguing plots, as in *The Lost Button* (2007, 2012) by Iren Rozdobudko (b. 1962), or with eccentric humour, as in *The Sarabande of Sara's Band* (2008, 2013) by Larysa Denysenko (b. 1973). The *Herstories* collection enables readers to sample short texts by other significant women writers of the first decade of the twenty-first century: Liudmyla Taran, Natalka Sniadanko, Dzvinka Matyash and Irena Karpa.

Ukrainian society's self-mobilisations to defend democracy – the Orange Revolution of 2004 and the Revolution of Dignity, or Euromaidan, of 2013–14 – were anticipated by a less familiar pro-democracy protest called the Revolution on the Granite (1990). This protest drives the plot of *Ivan and Phoebe* (2019, 2023) by poet and novelist Oksana Lutsyshyna (b. 1974), one of a number of Ukrainian writers who live abroad. Ivan, the novel's central figure, driven by hope and political conviction, joins the Revolution, only to surrender in the following years to disappointment, timidity and frustration – which he vents by psychologically abusing his wife Phoebe. Lutsyshyna's earlier novel *Love Life* (2016, 2024), the story of an asymmetrical love relationship in which the woman protagonist is abused by a self-serving, exploitative man, is also a complex discussion of virtue and the morality of the quest for self-fulfilment. An enduring theme of Lutsyshyna's oeuvre is the uncertain relationship between human experience and an intuited transcendental world, addressed urgently in such of her wartime poems as 'eastern europe is a pit of death' and 'he asks, don't help me'.

1965: Dissenting from the Party-State

In December 1965, the charismatic and eloquent literary critic Ivan Dziuba (1931–2022), the leading spokesperson of Ukrainian non-conformist intellectuals, sent a book-length memorandum to the heads of the Communist Party of Ukraine and the government of the Ukrainian Soviet Socialist Republic. The treatise, *Internationalism or Russification?*, was strikingly critical of the USSR's nationalities policy. Echoing Lenin's denunciation of Great Russian chauvinism, Dziuba condemned the privilege that Russian culture enjoyed over that of non-Russian nationalities: Russian-language print materials disproportionately outweighed their non-Russian counterparts, education promoted Russian culture and a Russocentric perspective on history, and in Ukraine, Russian was the language of prestige, while the use of Ukrainian was discouraged.

Internationalism or Russification? circulated underground through the *samvydav* (self-publishing) network and found its way abroad; beginning in 1968, translations into several languages were published. Meanwhile, Dziuba's speeches at events dedicated to Ukrainian culture aroused the authorities' suspicion. In 1965, at the Kyiv premiere of Sergei Parajanov's film *Shadows of Forgotten Ancestors*, Dziuba condemned the recent arrests of Ukrainian intellectuals. The following year, he spoke at a gathering to mark the twenty-fifth anniversary of the Nazi murders of Jews and others at Babyn Yar, accusing the Soviet state of failing to combat anti-Semitism just as it failed to abide by Leninist norms in its treatment of Ukraine and Ukrainian culture (*UD*: 29–33). Arrested in 1972, Dziuba was sentenced to a long imprisonment. To the dismay of many, he recanted. In the following years, he avoided controversy while continuing to write, often on the literatures of the Asian and Caucasian parts of the USSR. He came to the fore again as an advocate of Ukrainian language and culture during the period of *hlasnist* and was a revered public intellectual in independent Ukraine.

Dziuba and the group of poets and intellectuals who shared a desire to create an authentic Ukrainian culture and were critical of the practices of Soviet Communism – though not necessarily of Marxism–Leninism itself – came to be called the *shistdesiatnyky*, or 'Sixtiers' (see Figure 5). The core of the Sixtiers encompassed a relatively small number of key personalities. They included the literary critics Yevhen Sverstiuk (1928–2014), whose politically provocative

Figure 5 The Sixtiers, mid-1960s. From left, Orest Zilynsky, unknown, Mykola Vinhranovsky, Ivan Dziuba, Ivan Drach, Ivan Svitlychny, Lina Kostenko and Yevhen Sverstiuk. Photographer unknown. Reproduced by permission of the Museum of the Sixtiers.

cultural analyses are available in the collection *Clandestine Essays* (1976), and Ivan Svitlychny (1929–92). The poets included Lina Kostenko (b. 1930), Ivan Drach (1936–2018), Vasyl Symonenko (1935–63), Mykola Vinhranovsky (1936–2004) and Vitaly Korotych (b. 1936) as well as the slightly younger Ihor Kalynets (b. 1939) and Vasyl Stus (1938–85). The prose writers Valeriy Shevchuk and Volodymyr Drozd (1939–2003), the theatre director Les Taniuk (1938–2016) and the monumental painters Alla Horska (1929–70) and Viktor Zaretsky (1925–90) were also notable participants.

The Sixtiers belonged to a generation born in the 1930s, mainly in villages and small towns in Central and Eastern Ukraine. As children or teenagers, they experienced the violence and privation of war, German occupation and Soviet reconquest. Yet they also benefited from the social mobility that Soviet education offered young people of talent. Almost all received a higher education in the humanities. Most gravitated to Kyiv, where, brought together by shared values and dedication to Ukrainian culture, they were soon bound by personal friendship.

The phenomenon of the Sixtiers arose in the period of the 'Thaw', which followed Stalin's death in 1953 and his denunciation in 1956 by Nikita Khrushchev, the new leader of the Communist Party. It was a time of contradictory developments. Many political prisoners were rehabilitated and permitted to return from prison camp or exile. Some writers murdered by the regime could now be mentioned and even published. In the arts, the prohibition on formal innovation was relaxed somewhat, but adherence to party ideology remained compulsory. The status of the Ukrainian language took a blow in 1958 when, capitalising on the link between upward social mobility and assimilation to the dominant culture, the state allowed parents to choose to have children taught in Russian rather than their own language.

The Sixtiers achieved their greatest public resonance through poetry. The poet most sensational in his rejection of Soviet diction was Ivan Drach, whose poem cycle 'Knife in the Sun' (Drach 1978: 57–66) was published in 1961 in the official newspaper of the Writers' Union of the Ukrainian SSR. Excited by Yuri Gagarin's space flight, the work bristled with technological terms and startling images. Like much modernist poetry in the West, some of Drach's poems demanded intellectual effort for their decipherment; many, such as 'Sunflower' (Drach 1978: 7), impressed with the originality and precision of their vision.

The new poetry celebrated subjective experience. Mykola Vinhranovsky, an actor, film director and poet, created some of the Sixtiers' finest and most original love lyrics; the small selection of them in *100Y* gives only a hint of their delicacy and intimacy. Vitaly Korotych extolled individuality and specificity to the point of excoriating universals ('I spit on the words "general," "generally," "on the whole,"' *FUP*: 35), while Drach celebrated introspection as a condition of creativity ('Loneliness', *FUP*: 9).

Vasyl Symonenko, the most accessible and popular poet among the Sixtiers, on the other hand, articulated in 'Solitude' the burden of Robinson Crusoe-like spiritual isolation: 'Oh God! At least send me a foe, / If you don't want to send me a friend' (Symonenko 1975: 43). Symonenko used traditional metre and rhyme. His essentially Romantic sensibility is manifest in his tribute to love for homeland, 'Swans of Motherhood' (Symonenko 1975: 51), which became a popular song. His radicalism lay in the content of his poems, which circulated in *samvydav* and did much to shape the political image of the Sixtiers among émigré Ukrainians. Symonenko abhorred social unfairness. In 'Thief', he decried the poverty that drives an old farm worker to steal a bag of grain and the state propaganda that labels him a criminal (*FUP*: 73). In 'The Prophesy of 1917' (Symonenko 2017: 100), 'The Court', 'Choir of the Elders' and 'Monarchs' (*FUP*: 69, 77, 81), Symonenko condemned the Soviet system for, respectively, its betrayal of people's hopes for a better life, intolerance of new ideas, self-righteous claims to knowledge and demands for sycophantic praise of its sham humanity. Most provocative of all, however, was Symonenko's stance against colonialism. In 'To a Kurdish Brother', the stateless Kurds symbolise all peoples who are denied rights, not only to sovereignty but also to their own identity, by colonial masters: 'They did not come just to take all you own, / But for your name and language too.' The remedy is stark: 'Oh, Kurd, conserve your ammo, / But don't spare the lives of murderers' (Symonenko 2022). In addition to poetry, Symonenko authored a few short stories and a diary, published in English as *Rose Petal Wine* (1965, 2020).

In the poetry of Lina Kostenko of the late 1950s and early 1960s, generalised reflections on the human condition often concealed barbs against contemporary Soviet reality. Kostenko was the most visual of the Sixtiers, adept at vividly picturing natural phenomena (as in 'Stars' and 'The Rains'; *FUP*: 49, 51). Her eye for the unexpected metaphor caused her trouble when the poem 'Ferns' (1957, *FUP*: 45) became controversial for seeing ferns in a forest clearing as 'green birds'.

Symonenko died in 1963 at the age of twenty-eight. Drach and Vinhranovsky managed to keep publishing through the reactionary 1970s, the former re-emerging to play an important role in the Ukrainian national movement in the late 1980s. Korotych moved to Moscow in the 1980s and became editor-in-chief of the journal *Ogonek*, turning it into a leading mouthpiece for Gorbachev's liberalisation policies. Lina Kostenko, like the prose writer Valeriy Shevchuk, was unpublished for much of the 1970s. In 1979, her historical novel in verse

Marusia Churai (1979) appeared. Set in the mid-seventeenth century in the sovereign Cossack state that is a key symbol in Ukraine's interrupted tradition of independence, the work, both patriotic and feminist, tells of the semi-legendary songwriter Marusia Churai. Marusia's tragedy is that she, a pillar of national culture, is betrayed by both her male lover and a judicial system created by men.

Lina Kostenko's later poems appeared in English in her *Selected Poetry: Wanderings of the Heart* (1990) and *Landscapes of Memory* (2002). In 2010, at the age of eighty, the grand dame of Ukrainian poetry published her first novel, *Diary of a Ukrainian Madman* (2010, excerpted in *Herstories*: 410–21), a satirical work critical of Ukrainian society and politics before the Orange Revolution.

The years 1972–73 saw a new wave of arrests of Ukrainian intellectuals. Its victims included the poets Ihor Kalynets and Vasyl Stus. Kalynets had one collection of poems officially published before falling under suspicion as a dangerous dissenter. The manuscript of Stus's first collection was rejected by publishers after he supported Dziuba's protest at the premiere of *Shadows of Forgotten Ancestors*. Thereafter, their works circulated in *samvydav* and, spirited out of the USSR, were published abroad. Kalynets and Stus composed significant parts of their poetic opus in prison or labour camp. Both created bodies of work of philosophical and aesthetic distinction, of which the extant English-language translations give only a slight idea.

Kalynets's opus is stylistically diverse. While the bulk of it is in unpunctuated free verse resistant to easy understanding in the manner of much modernist poetry, there are also many poems in traditional forms. The world view articulated in Kalynets's poetry evolves from pagan pantheism to explicit Christian religiosity. The poems of this later phase are exercises in the prayerful praise of the God-created world by means of the depiction and admiration of its parts.

The poetry of Kalynets that is available in English – four cycles from the collection 'Summing up Silence' (Kalynets 2014) and the collection *Crowning the Scarecrow* (1972, 1990) – belongs to his early period. The lyrical subject is drawn to a religious view of the world, but does not yet discount the secular perspective; vacillation between the two gives rise to 'Verses about Uncertainty' (*100Y*: 419–27). The ten poems that comprise the cycle 'Threnody for One More Way of the Cross' (Kalynets 2014: 177–86) tell of Christ's agonising walk to Calvary and His crucifixion as a prelude to salvation, but are at the same time allegorical of the plight of Ukraine. Likewise, Kalynets's inquiries into the nuances of erotic love in *Crowning the Scarecrow* are explorations of physical and spiritual connection to a human Other, but also of the bond between the self and a world beyond experience.

While Kalynets's poetry underplays the tribulations of its author in the Soviet penal system, images of incarceration pervade Stus's later works. Prison, visualised through the geometric form of the square (the barred window, the four walls of the cell), symbolises suffering, deprivation of freedom and, more generally, human limitation; the circle, embodied in the movement of celestial bodies or the roundness of organic forms (the flower, the egg or the belly of the pregnant woman), alludes to the possibility of harmony and even beauty. Of the poems by Stus that have been translated into English, the majority are from the poet's earlier years, when his focus was on the experience of solitude and isolation within an alien and unforgiving world – as in 'Meditation' or 'And Thus I Live: An Ape Among the Apes' (Stus 1987: 39, 125).

What was articulated with startling originality in Stus's poetry was also embodied in his life, which has become a modern parable of Ukrainian martyrdom. Stus's first penal sentence (for 'anti-Soviet agitation and propaganda') was for five years of imprisonment followed by three years' exile. He served it in full and, on returning to Kyiv in 1979, joined the Ukrainian Helsinki Accords Monitoring Group, which dissidents had established to record and publicise Soviet breaches of human rights. In 1980, he was arrested again and sentenced to ten years' hard labour and five years of exile. This he did not survive, dying in 1985 in a prison camp in the Perm region of Russia. In 1989, his mortal remains, together with those of Yurii Lytvyn and Oleksa Tykhy, Ukrainian political prisoners who had perished in the same camp, were returned to Kyiv. The great public resonance of this event both reflected and advanced the resurgence of Ukrainian national consciousness in the years preceding independence.

Compared to the ethical blaze of the new poetry, the gleam of the new prose was subdued. Nonetheless, the short stories of the young Valeriy Shevchuk mentioned in the preceding section and works of similar genre and spirit by Yevhen Hutsalo (1937–95), Volodymyr Drozd (1939–2003) and Hryhir Tiutiunnyk (1931–80) were novel phenomena in Soviet Ukrainian literature, insofar as they generally avoided or at least minimised the ideological pathos that had been compulsory for their predecessors. The trail of innovation in Ukrainian prose had been blazed by the renowned filmmaker Alexander Dovzhenko (1894–1956). In 1955, Dovzhenko wrote in the USSR's central literary newspaper *Literaturnaia gazeta* of the need to expand the creative limits of Socialist Realism. Soon afterwards, he published his autobiographical 'cinema story', as he labelled it, *The Enchanted Desna* (1956, 1982). The work lovingly portrayed the author's childhood in a pre-revolutionary northern Ukrainian village with its eccentric characters, traditional lifeways, cuisine, superstitions and religious beliefs – a childhood surrounded by animals, lush vegetable gardens and fields, and spoilt only by the incursion of school (conducted in a foreign and barely understood language, Russian).

The younger generation followed suit. Hutsalo's stories of the early 1960s almost all had villages for their setting. Many were delicate explorations of the psyche of children or teenagers as they encountered the complexities of maturity; some, like 'Bathed in Lovage Root', gave nuanced and understated depictions of the early stirrings of erotic desire (Hutsalo 1974: 153–65); one, 'A Sea Story', stood out for its menacing narration of an attempt by an elderly paedophile to abduct a young girl (*MUSS*: 173–85). Tiutiunnyk, who was not part of the Sixtiers' friendship group, was both acclaimed and criticised for the grim veracity of his representation of life in the Soviet village. A selection of his work appeared in English as *Cool Mint* (1986), years after his death by suicide.

Drozd's stories of the same period explored the psychological complexities of life in the post–Second World War village. Darker and more focussed on hardship and privation than Hutsalo's stories, they were also technically more varied and adventurous. Drozd experimented with the narrator's point of view, telling stories from the perspective, for example, of a horse or a house goblin ('The Seasons', written in 1970, 2007c). Some of his stories, especially later ones, aimed to generate interest from unexpected twists of the plot ('Fame', 1982, 2007b) or from irreverent extrapolations of religious motifs ('Everything All Over Again', 1988, 2007a).

Hutsalo and Drozd continued writing prolifically in the following decades, shifting emphasis from short stories to novels. These longer works, however, did not attract as much interest as their early publications. What did cause excitement in literary circles was the seeming ideological about-face of Oles Honchar (1918–95), a writer of the first magnitude in the Soviet establishment. His war-themed trilogy, *Standard-Bearers* (1946/1948, 1950), had the personal approval of Stalin and was the foundation of his successful career. And yet, in his novel *The Cathedral* (1968, 1989), Honchar deviated from Party orthodoxy. The Socialist Realist novel standardly contained a 'positive hero' who embodied Party values. *The Cathedral* has a positive hero, but he is an environmental activist who also fights to preserve from demolition a cathedral built in Cossack times – an advocacy that in real life would have been condemned as nationalist. The novel was sharply criticised and remained unmentionable for two decades, although the affair had no serious repercussions for Honchar. Then, republished in 1987 as *hlasnist* gathered momentum, *The Cathedral* bolstered Honchar's credentials as a champion of Ukrainian national culture.

A text that radically challenged the formal, as well as ideological, conventions of Soviet prose was *Cataract* (1971, 1976) written by the journalist

Mykhailo Osadchy (1936–94) in 1968 between his two terms in prison camps. A work of non-fiction (its subject matter is Osadchy's experience of arrest, interrogation and imprisonment), *Cataract* displays features associated with literary modernism: a fragmented narrative with jumbled chronology, absurdist motivations and devices of alienation that underscore the disparity between an object and its representation. The text repeatedly refers to the Western modernist tradition, explicitly mentioning Surrealism, Imaginism and Impressionism, and invoking Franz Kafka and James Joyce by name. The argument underlying the work's anti-realism is that what appears grotesque and absurd in fact faithfully reflects Soviet reality.

Two writers went beyond criticism of the practice of Soviet communism to question the very principles of Marxism–Leninism: the first two leaders of the Ukrainian Helsinki Group, Mykola Rudenko (1920–2004) and Oles Berdnyk (1926–2003). In the novel *Orlova Balka* (Eagle's Ravine, written in 1970, published in 1982), Rudenko gave literary form to his rejection of the labour theory of value in favour of a return to the eighteenth-century physiocratic view that wealth originates in the capacity of nature to generate organic growth. Berdnyk's works of fantasy, science fiction and futurological speculation reflected his view of humans as immortal and potentially omnipotent spiritual beings, a notion in evidence in the short works collected in *Apostle of Immortality* (1984).

Among the dissidents who were permitted or forced to emigrate from the Ukrainian SSR were the Russian-language journalist and writer Viktor Nekrasov (1911–87) and the poet Moisei Fishbein (1946–2020). Nekrasov, author of *Front-line Stalingrad* (1946, 1962), became an associate editor of the Russian émigré journal *Kontinent* in Paris. Fishbein's work in the Ukrainian-language service of Radio Liberty in Germany and his publications in *Suchasnist* brought him into contact with members of the New York Group, a cohort of poets of approximately the same generation as the Sixtiers. The handful of Fishbein's poems included in *100Y* highlights one of the main themes of his work, the traumatic history of Ukrainian Jews.

Members of the New York Group were united by a shared commitment to the modernist sensibility, though they differed in the ways in which they brought that sensibility to expression. The New York of their collective name was a place more symbolic than geographical. New York was home to Bohdan Boychuk (1927–2017), Yuriy Tarnawsky (b. 1934) and Patricia Kylyna (Patricia Nell Warren, who during her association with the Group wrote in Ukrainian; 1936–2019), while Bohdan Rubchak (1935–2018) lived in Chicago, Wira Wowk (1926–2022) in Rio de Janeiro and Emma Andievska (b. 1931) in Munich.

A selection of Boychuk's urban, often erotically charged, verse was published in English as *Memories of Love* (1989). Rubchak's complex, ornamental and erudite poetry is sampled in his *Songs of Love, Songs of Death, Songs of the Moon* (2020). Tarnawsky writes poetry and prose in both Ukrainian and English. His verse, sometimes minimalist and sometimes dense with richly visual surreal images, experiments with ever new forms (*100Y*: 369–75); he is the author of numerous volumes of experimental prose in English, including the early *Meningitis* (1978) and the five 'mininovels' comprising *Like Blood in Water* (2007). Wira Wowk's sense of the sacred in the world, her respectful attention to the people and the natural environment of Brazil and her capacity for aphoristic laconicism are illustrated in an all-too-brief selection in *100Y*. Patricia Nell Warren in the later and larger part of her literary career wrote in English and was noted for pioneering the theme of same-sex attraction in the novel *The Front Runner* (1974). Her Ukrainian-language poetry shared the surrealist expressive modes characteristic of much of the Group's work. Emma Andievska, the most prolific poet of the group, frequently combines traditional stanzas and metres with the vivid and grotesque imagery that also characterises her paintings. Her prose works, of which *A Novel about a Good Person* (1973, 2022) is an example, are both exercises in philosophical, especially ethical, reflection and examples of syntactical extremism: their sentences, scrupulously grammatical, continue for pages.

1933: Death and Life with Totalitarianism

On 13 May 1933, Mykola Khvylovy (1893–1933), the uncrowned king of revolutionary Ukrainian prose and cultural polemic, invited two friends to visit him in his apartment: the Communist Party activist and writer Oles Dosvitnii (1891–1934) and Ukraine's most eminent playwright Mykola Kulish (1892–1937). Troubled by the Party's increasingly repressive measures against cultural workers, they discussed the recent arrest of the poet Mykhailo Yalovy (1895–1937). As they were about to part, Khvylovy went into the next room and shot himself. His suicide note expressed incomprehension at the persecution of 'us, the most dedicated communists'. Dosvitnii would be executed less than a year later, and Yalovy and Kulish in 1937. Thirty-four writers who published mainly in Ukrainian are mentioned in this section. Seven either emigrated or did not live in Soviet Ukraine. Of the remaining twenty-seven, nineteen were imprisoned, and of these, fifteen met their death by execution. Eight were shot on a single day, 3 November 1937, in the forest of Sandarmokh in northern Russia. These victims of Stalin's terror are often collectively referred to as 'the Executed Renaissance'.

Khvylovy's death in the spring of 1933 coincided with the peak of the great famine, mourned in Ukraine as the Holodomor, whose victims numbered in the millions. The Holodomor, a result of deliberate state policy, was a topic prohibited in Soviet public discourse until 1987. What preceded the Holodomor – enforced collectivisation of agriculture and the deportation to inhospitable parts of the Soviet Union of peasants deemed, implausibly, to be 'wealthy' – did become the subject matter of Soviet Ukrainian literature. But with few exceptions, writers followed the ideological directives of the state and joined the propaganda campaign against the peasantry – just as the filmmaker Alexander Dovzhenko did in his celebrated film *Zemlia* (Earth, 1930).

The Soviet Ukrainian literary milieu of the 1920s and early 1930s was characterised by a proliferation of literary groupings that strove to outdo each other in proving their commitment to the revolutionary goals of the Communist Party. The variety and number of these groups reflected the burgeoning of Ukrainian literary and cultural activity that was one of the side effects of a political strategy adopted by Lenin and the Communist Party in the early 1920s. The revolution of 1917 in many of the non-Russian parts of the Russian Empire took national form and resulted in the proclamation of independent nation-states, which the Bolshevik regime subsequently defeated by force of arms. The fact that the Soviet state was established in 1922 not as a unitary entity but as a Union of Soviet Socialist Republics was a concession to the strength of these national movements. To address the paucity of communist leaders drawn from the non-Russian nationalities, the Party introduced a policy of 'indigenisation'. Education in the national languages was mandated, use of these languages by state officials was encouraged and cultural workers competent in their use were recruited to promote the Party ideology. Furthermore, Russian chauvinist attitudes toward non-Russian peoples and cultures were officially condemned. Called 'Ukrainisation' in Ukraine, the policy was embraced by most intellectuals, including many who had previously worked and fought for Ukraine's independence. Among its foremost advocates were the writers shown in Figure 6. Conforming to Party direction seemed at first a small price to pay for the promise of a blossoming of Ukrainian culture.

Khvylovy came to Kharkiv, the capital of Soviet Ukraine, in 1921. He captured attention at first with his poetry, then with his short stories, of which the most sensational and most in tune with the aesthetics of European Expressionism was 'My Being' (*MUSS*: 115–46). During the war to impose Soviet power a young member of a revolutionary tribunal encounters his mother who, having become a nun, now represents a reactionary social force. Should he retain his doctrinaire purity, and execute her? Or yield to filial instinct, and spare her? He chooses the former. The extremity of the situation is matched by the alienating technical devices used to depict it: fragments of narrative alternate with flashbacks and flights of imagination; lines of dialogue are preceded by the

Figure 6 Ukrainian writers, 1923. Front row, from left: first, Maskym Rylsky; third, Mykola Khvylovy; fourth, Maik Yohansen. Second row, from left: fifth, Pavlo Tychyna; sixth, Pavlo Fylypovych. Third row, from left: second, Mykola Zerov; third, Mykhailo Drai-Khmara. Public domain image.

name of the speaker, as in the text of a play; sentences are pared to the minimum required to communicate meaning.

The formation of a new, young and progressive Ukrainian intelligentsia is the substance of conversations among the characters of Khvylovy's novel *The Woodcocks* (1927; excerpted in *BTS*: 15–67). The novel shared the argumentative quality of Khvylovy's most consequential writings: his polemical essays. In the controversy called the 'Literary Discussion' of 1925–28, Khvylovy defended the ideal of a Ukrainian modern high literary art anchored in European literary tradition against advocates of a utilitarian view of culture as a tool for the implementation of Party objectives.

Khvylovy's invective and satirical mockery were unparalleled. He was a master of the laconic formulation of key issues. The title of his pamphlet 'Ukraine or Little Russia?' (Khvylovy 1986: 226–32) encapsulated its message: it condemned past colonial attitudes toward Ukraine and their persistence into the present, and held up instead the vision of an ascendant Ukraine as a source of revolutionary modernity and an inspiration for the 'Asiatic renaissance' that was destined to transform the Eurasian continent. The three-word slogan most commonly ascribed to Khvylovy, 'Away from Moscow!', though an apt paraphrase of his anti-colonial message, is nowhere to be found in his works.

Borys Antonenko-Davydovych (1899–1984) in his novel *Duel* (1927, 1986) addressed a theme similar to that of Khvylovy's 'My Being', but without Khvylovy's Expressionist pyrotechnics. The central character of *Duel*, a communist assertive of his Ukrainian identity, carries out Party directives even more punitively than Bolshevik norms demand in order to prove his loyalty to the real powerholders: unreconstructed devotees of the imperial idea and the Russian culture that nourishes it. After returning from terms of imprisonment and exile that lasted, with one year's break, from 1935 to 1957, Antonenko-Davydovych wrote the novel *Behind the Curtain* (1963, 1980), in which the central character learns late in life to regret neglecting his all-forgiving mother. In the Soviet context, it was difficult to read this plot otherwise than as an allegorical condemnation of indifference to one's nation.

In the 1920s, revolutionary egalitarianism combined with the imperatives of Ukrainisation to propel gifted young people from Ukrainian-speaking villages into education and then into urban careers. The prose writer Valerian Pidmohylny (1901–37), a representative of this social phenomenon, made it the theme of his novel *Misto* (The City, 1928), a psychologically subtle account of a young man's at first tentative, and then increasingly confident, steps as he learns to navigate Kyiv and experiences success as a writer. Pidmohylny's *City* was followed by *A Little Touch of Drama* (1930, 1972), another urban novel about young people's complex quests for erotic and social fulfilment against the background of Ukrainisation in newly sovietised Kyiv.

The short stories and excerpts from longer works gathered in the collection *Before the Storm* (BTS) are illustrative of the thematic concerns and writing styles of the period's major authors. In many cases, these works also reveal writers' more or less daring attempts to smuggle criticism of the new order into their texts. Ivan Senchenko (1901–75) is acerbic in his 'Notes of a Flunky', a parodic manual for cynics intent on flourishing under Soviet rule (171–8). Hryhorii Epik (1901–37) in 'The Radio Ham' (69–100) satirises the bureaucrat terrified of arrest despite faithfully echoing official dogma. In the short story 'Kostryha' by Arkadii Liubchenko (1899–1945), it is not clear who deserves moral opprobrium – the peasant who hides his grain from the state, or the state that confiscates it from him (111–6). In 'Politics', Hryhorii Kosynka (1899–1934) appears to invite readers to sympathise with an incorruptible communist who confiscates a valuable asset – a bull – from a prosperous peasant and is lynched for doing so. But at the same time Kosynka paints a grim picture of the fierce resentment that the Party's drive to collectivise agriculture encounters in the village (159–70). Ostap Vyshia (1889–1956), a master of the humorous feuilleton and of the self-deprecating irony that is on display in 'My Autobiography' (233–46), divides his satirical barbs between safe targets – small entrepreneurs tolerated under Lenin's New Economic Policy – and less safe ones, such as zealots of Russian imperialism. A collection of Vyshnia's stories was published in English as *Hard Times* (1981).

Among Ukrainian literature's most mysterious figures was Viktor Petrov (1894–1969). A philosopher, anthropologist, literary scholar and very probably an agent of the Soviet secret service, Petrov was also a gifted author of fiction and fictionalised biography that he published under the pseudonym Viktor Domontovych. His prose of the 1920s included novels based on the intimate lives of two prominent Ukrainian nineteenth-century intellectuals, Mykola Kostomarov and Panteleimon Kulish, as well as the fictional *Doctor Seraficus* (written in 1929; 1947, excerpted in *BTS*: 187–92). In these psychologically nuanced works, convoluted relationships and repressed eroticism take shape in conversations among characters whom the omniscient narrator generally treats with irony. Petrov escaped the repressions of the 1930s almost unscathed. In Germany, after the Second World War, he became active in émigré literary circles and penned *On Shaky Ground* (1948, 2024), a novel in which the plot is a vehicle for debates about the aesthetics of modernism. In 1949, he mysteriously disappeared, only to resurface years later in the USSR.

One of the very few women in the overwhelmingly masculine (and often masculinist) Ukrainian literary culture of the 1930s was Zinaida Tulub (1890–1964), a trained historian. Like many of her generation (including, of those mentioned in this section, Fylypovych, Sosiura, Yohansen and Yanovsky), she began writing in Russian but chose to participate in the Ukrainian literary revival. Her major work was the historical novel *Liudolovy* (The People Hunters, 1934/1937), set in the early seventeenth century and having real historical figures among its characters: the Cossack hetman Petro Konashevych-Sahaidachnyi and Roksolana – captive, trafficked woman and, ultimately, power-wielding wife of the Ottoman sultan Suleiman the Magnificent. After returning from two decades of imprisonment and exile, Tulub wrote *The Exile* (1964, 2015), a biographical novel about Taras Shevchenko. No less notable than Tulub's choice of identity was the decision by Leonid Pervomaisky (1908–73) to continue to identify as Jewish while making Ukrainian the language of his literary self-expression. Continuously prolific as a writer of prose and poetry from the 1920s onward, Pervomaisky is known in English through a small number of anthologised lyric poems (*UP*: 481; *ASUP*: 194–204; *100Y*: 310–5).

Yuriy Yanovsky (1902–54) is best known for *The Ship's Master* (1928, excerpted in *BTS*: 117–24), a novel set in Odesa that reflects Yanovsky's Romantic enthusiasm for the sea. The plot concerns an artistic undertaking excitingly modern at the time: the making of a film, as well as the associated adventures and erotic intrigues. The short novel *Bayhorod* (1927, 2018) drew on personal experience: a teenager during the wars following the Revolution, Yanovsky witnessed the defence of his native city by self-organised citizens against an anarchist armed group. The revolutionary wars were also the settings of another two of his novels, *Chotyry shabli* (Four Swords, 1930) and *The Horsemen* (1935, 1989). Though acclaimed, neither achieved the international fame enjoyed by *Red Cavalry* (1926, 1929), a Russian-language collection of narratives by Odesa-born Isaac Babel (1894–1940) on the war between Bolshevik and Polish forces fought on Ukrainian territory in 1920.

Far removed from the traditions of realism was the work of Maik Yohansen (1895–1937), especially his eccentric and whimsically titled novel *The Journey of the Learned Doctor Leonardo and His Future Lover, the Beauteous Alceste, to the Switzerland of Slobozhanshchyna* (1928/1932, 2021). The hero begins as a Spanish would-be revolutionary assassin, but finds himself inexplicably transformed into a sentimental minor communist functionary in the Ukrainian countryside. As the latter, he travels with Alceste, the object of his amorous hopes, down a river through the beguiling landscapes of Slobozhanshchyna, the historical region centred on Kharkiv. The depiction of the journey embodies the author's capriciously proclaimed intent to make landscape, not character, the focus of his novel.

Notwithstanding affinities between Yohansen's experimental aesthetics and the theory and practice of the Futurist movement, Yohansen never joined any Ukrainian Futurist organisations. These were mostly projects of the movement's leader in Ukraine, the poet Mykhail Semenko (1892–1937). Semenko had commenced his iconoclastic career as early as 1914, publishing poetry whose deliberate barbarity was designed to outrage both traditionalists and adepts of *fin-de-siècle* aestheticism. Especially shocking was Semenko's attack on the authority of Shevchenko. The Futurist movement in Ukraine also included the poets and prose writers Geo Shkurupii (1903–37) and Oleksa Slisarenko (1891–1937). In line with the 1909 *Manifesto of Futurism* authored by Futurism's Italian progenitor Filippo Tommaso Marinetti, Ukrainian futurists were enthusiasts of the ideas and images of speed, technology and youth. They also embraced stimuli from Dadaism, surrealism and the avant-garde in general. The stylistic particularities of futurist poetry – its love for neologism, unconventional syntax and the fragmentation of words into their component syllables and letters – are evident in the translations included in anthologies (*UP*: 378–85; *100Y*: 185–92), as well as in the many literal translations of quotations interspersed through Oleh Ilnytzkyj's scholarly study of the movement (Ilnytzkyj 1997).

Futurist features were in evidence in the early poetry of Mykola Bazhan (1904–83; see Bazhan 2020), but by the late 1920s he had developed a saturated, hyperbolic and often grotesque diction that earned him the label of an Expressionist poet. A long poem of 1929 illustrates this strident voice: 'Hoffmann's Nights' constructs a characteristically Romantic contrast, not without contemporary allusion, between the power of unfettered creativity and the limitations that mundane existence places upon the artist (*100Y*: 20–9). Bazhan survived the purges; his prolific, ideologically compliant but nonetheless exciting poetry written during and after the Second World War is well represented in *ASUP* (131–58).

Volodymyr Sosiura (1898–1965) merged a Romantic sensibility with revolutionary fervour and patriotism, both Ukrainian and Soviet. The narrative poem *Red Winter* (1922; *ASUP*: 81–4) established his popularity, which he maintained with a steady output of accessible, mellifluous verse, interspersing love and nature poetry (e.g., 'No One Loved So Before', *100Y*: 211) with praise of his native Donbas and, at times of war, dutiful calls to arms ('A Letter to My Fellow Countrymen', *ASUP*: 87–9). Echoes of a different, darker, Romanticism are audible in the poetry of Yevhen Pluzhnyk (1898–1936), whose lyrical verse dwells on the themes of solitude and death, often drawing its nature imagery from twilight or the night ('Night . . . A Boat – Like a Silver Bird!', *ASUP*: 162). The poem 'At night they led him to a firing squad' (*100Y*: 245) proved sadly prophetic for Pluzhnyk and for much of his generation.

Against the mainstream of politicised cultural activity, a group of five Kyiv intellectuals, four of them literary scholars, cultivated what they saw as timeless aesthetic ideals: in place of excited formlessness, harmony and balance; in place of expressive improvisation, craftsmanship informed by erudition; in place of passionate urges to build a classless future, a vision of the continuity of civilisation. Mykola Zerov (1890–1937), Pavlo Fylypovych (1891–1937), Mykhailo Drai-Khmara (1889–1939), Yurii Klen (pseudonym of Oswald Burghardt, 1891–1947) and Maksym Rylsky (1895–1964) were dubbed 'Neoclassicists' by their adversaries; they embraced the name, appropriate as it was to their shared love of traditional poetic forms and themes from classical antiquity. Representative of their aloofness from the ambient cultural noise was Zerov's poem 'Aristarchus', in which the librarian of Alexandria ignores the 'bards and poetasters' swarming his city and 'immerse[s] himself in the Homeric text' (*UP*: 370). The poetry of the Neoclassicists is relatively well anthologised in English (*100Y*: 142–75; *UP*: 338–72 and 386–95; Slavutych 1956: 21–30). Zerov, Fylypovych and Drai-Khmara were murdered in the purges; Burghardt emigrated in 1931; Rylsky survived, paying with panegyrics to the Party for the right to continue creating his formally polished verse. With two other masters of translation into Ukrainian, Mykola Lukash (1919–88) and Hryhorii Kochur (1908–94), Rylsky contributed much to the refinement of the

Ukrainian literary language. Late in life, he used his standing in the literary establishment to soften the attacks of Soviet officialdom on the Sixtiers. An anthology of his pre-1929 poetry is available in English (Rylsky 2017), as is a volume documenting the life and works of Drai-Khmara, including his poetry (Asher 1983).

Even more remote than the Neoclassicists from the conception of literature as politics by other means was Volodymyr Svidzinsky (1885–1941), a selection of whose poems has appeared in translation (Svidzinsky 2017). Svidzinsky's small oeuvre creates a deeply private lyrical world of calm observation and meditation on the relationship of the poetic self to nature ('Sudden Snow Fell on Green Branches', 39), the beloved ('Don't Say Anything, Darling', 61; 'Straw Scattered All Over the Courtyards', 143), time ('The Pendulum Is Tired', 151) and the art of poetry ('The Poet's Soul', 159). Concentration of thought and image characterise Svidzinsky's work: some of his poems are no more than a few lines long.

One of the most important sites of Ukrainian modernist experimentation in the 1920s and 1930s was theatre. In Kharkiv, the Berezil Theatre led by Les Kurbas (1887–1937) mounted Expressionist productions with abstract Constructivist stage sets. Berezil's repertoire included the dangerously controversial plays of Mykola Kulish. The central character in Kulish's tragicomedy *The People's Malachi* (1928, *AMUD*: 72–124) is possessed by a vocation to reform humanity. In this, he resembles true believers of the Communist Party. The analogy is risky, however: Malachi is insane. *Myna Mazailo* (1929) satirised both reactionary philistine opponents to Ukrainisation and its overenthusiastic advocates. *Sonata Pathétique* (1930, 1975; also *AMUD*: 130–88) dramatized interactions among ideological adversaries in the post-revolutionary wars: champions of Ukrainian independence, the Bolshevik revolution and the restoration of the Russian Empire. Too provocative for any Ukrainian stage, the play ran in Moscow and Leningrad in 1931–32. Also available in English is Kulish's *Blight* (1927, 1996).

While the Ukrainian SSR and especially its capital until 1934, Kharkiv, was the centre of gravity of Ukrainian literary life, about a quarter of Ukraine fell within the post–First World War boundaries of Poland, Czechoslovakia and Romania. Bohdan Ihor Antonych (1909–37) was born in the Lemko region. This westernmost promontory of Ukrainian ethnolinguistic territory was at first part of Austria-Hungary and then of the Polish Republic. Antonych developed in his poetry a vision of the universe as a grandiose spatial and temporal continuum in which the sun, stars and moon have as much presence as a grain of barley, a fish, an insect or, for that matter, a poet ('A Grain of Barley', Antonych 1977: 34). Capturing phenomena of nature in images of remarkable novelty and aptness, Antonych's poetry places them into great cycles of evolution and decay. Mammoths are fossils today; motor cars will be in the future ('Dead Automobiles', Antonych 2010: 156). The titles of some of Antonych's collections (e.g., *The Great Harmony* or *The Green Gospel*) and individual poems ('A Song on the Indestructibility of Matter', Antonych 2010: 110) are intimations of his pantheist philosophy.

Many intellectuals associated with the Ukrainian People's Republic or other independent Ukrainian state formations in 1917–21 emigrated to Poland, Germany or Czechoslovakia. Between the world wars, Prague became the main centre of cultural life for Ukrainian émigrés. Among them was Oleksandr Oles (pseudonym of Oleksandr Kandyba, 1878–1944), whose poetry had enjoyed popularity since the publication in 1907 of his first collection, *Z zhurboiu radist obnialas* (Joy and Sorrow Embraced). The title poem, as well as the frequently anthologised 'Asters' (*100Y*: 119), display the musicality, classical forms and nostalgic tone characteristic of Oles's verse; its patriotic side is in evidence in 'How Glorious: To See a Reborn Nation' (*UP*: 313). Other poets were similarly affected by Ukraine's achievement and subsequent loss of independence, and similarly traditionalist in form: Yevhen Malaniuk (1897–1968; samples of his poetry are in *UP*: 411–5 and *100Y*: 226–33), and the feminist polemicist Olena Teliha (1907–42). Active in the Ukrainian nationalist movement, during the Nazi occupation, Teliha returned to Kyiv where she was arrested by the Gestapo and executed. A collection of her poetry is available in English (Teliha 1977). Among the many novels of Ulas Samchuk (1905–87) was *Maria* (1934, 2011), the life story of a woman who endures the Holodomor and the miseries that preceded it. The theme of the Holodomor, untouchable in the Ukrainian SSR, would also be addressed, on the basis of personal observation and testimonies collected in the 1940s, by another émigré poet and writer, Vasyl Barka (1908–2003). His *Zhovtyi kniaz* (The Yellow Prince, 1962/2008), a philosophically and stylistically challenging work, still awaits translation into English.

The territory of today's Ukraine in the 1920s and 1930s was home to numerous writers working in other languages and within other traditions than the Ukrainian. Bruno Schulz (1892–1942), author of the short story collections *The Street of Crocodiles* (1934, 1963) and *Sanatorium Under the Sign of the Hourglass* (1937, 1979) and regarded as one of the foremost prose writers of Polish interwar modernism, was born and lived in Drohobych. Of Jewish background, he was shot dead by a Nazi officer on the streets of his home city. Alongside Isaak Babel, Ilya Ilf (1897–1937) and Yevgeny Petrov (1902–42) were members of what has become known as the Odesa School. Their jointly authored satirical novels, *The Twelve Chairs* (1928, 1961) and *The Little Golden Calf* (1931, 1932), written in Russian, helped create the apologetic image of a benign Soviet culture of everyday life.

In the late 1920s, the turbulent diversity of Soviet Ukrainian literary life began to dissolve as the Party took steps to bring all cultural activity under its control. In April 1932, the literary organisations still extant were abolished and replaced by a single Writers' Union with branches in the Union republics. In 1934, this entity convened for its first congress and accepted Socialist Realism as the artistic doctrine governing Soviet literary production. Soviet literature would now display a set of common features. Imaginative writing would support the objectives of the Communist Party. The USSR and its leadership would be portrayed only in a positive light. History would be represented as a succession of class struggles. Literary works would be intelligible to ordinary members of Soviet society, which in practice meant that nineteenth-century realism was instated as the binding stylistic norm. It went without saying that, in depictions of relations between the Soviet nationalities, the Russian people would be shown to play the leading and progressive role.

1918: The National Revolution

February 1917 saw the revolution in Petrograd that ended the autocratic rule of the tsar. In the non-Russian parts of the Russian Empire, it accelerated the transformation of national movements into movements for state independence: independence would be proclaimed, if only briefly maintained, by Ukraine, Belarus, the Crimean Tatars, the Don Cossacks, Georgia, Armenia, Azerbaijan and a number of proto-states in Central Asia. From March 1917, governmental authority over Ukrainian lands quickly passed to the Central Rada, or Council, in Kyiv. It was a time of mass demonstrations, public oratory and revolutionary (at times utopian) social legislation. Initially, there was no formal break with Russia. After the Bolshevik coup d'état of October 1917, however, it became clear that the new regime intended to destroy Ukrainian autonomy by military force. The Rada declared the full independence of the Ukrainian People's Republic on 22 January 1918, when Bolshevik troops were already on the verge of entering Kyiv.

By comparison with its predecessor, 1918 was a sombre year for Ukrainians. The First World War was still in progress. The Rada concluded a peace treaty with the Central Powers, securing the help of Germany and Austria-Hungary to drive out the Bolsheviks. The new allies, interested in access to Ukrainian grain, soon began acting as occupiers. They supported a conservative coup by a Ukrainian general whose government did not survive the withdrawal of the German troops after the surrender of the Central Powers in November. The Ukrainian People's Republic, re-established, faced hostile military action by the Bolsheviks, Poland, White armies seeking to restore the empire, and an array of warlords. By the end of 1921, Ukrainian military resistance to Bolshevik occupation had ceased.

In the course of 1918, a slim volume of poetry by Pavlo Tychyna (1891–1967) was published in Kyiv. *Soniashni kliarnety* (Sunny Clarinets) was an immediate critical success, earning praise for its musicality and its fusion of visual and aural imagery – features that led to Tychyna's early poetry being seen as part of the Europe-wide Symbolist movement. Such poems by Tychyna as 'Not Zeus, Not Pan' (Tychyna 2000: 30) announced a cosmology and an ethics: their beguiling harmonies and their visual world of brightness and clarity corresponded to the idea of a sacred unity of self, others and the universe. The poems' appeal to love as charity, forgiveness and generosity echoed the pathos of the eighteenth-century philosopher Hryhorii Skovoroda, to whom Tychyna devoted a long poem in 1922. The closing poem of *Sunny Clarinets*, 'The Golden Hum' (dated 1917, Tychyna 2000: 125–35), was a paean to the Kyiv of the national revolution, resounding with the clangour of church bells, surmounted by a sky full of sun and doves and radiant as the city had been when its hills and river received the legendary blessing of the Apostle Andrew. By contrast, the collection *Instead of Sonnets and Octaves* (1920) reflected on the new, darker phases of the revolution. *In the Orchestra of the Cosmos* (1921) was a series of pantheistic meditations on the presence of Spirit within matter and on the smallness, yet dignity, of the human being in the universe and in history.

In 1934, as Stalinist repressions intensified, Tychyna published a collection titled *Partiia vede* (The Party Leads); henceforth, he would produce versified Party dogma. Outside the USSR, he was almost universally regarded as having capitulated to the regime, with catastrophic results for the value of the work he produced in the second half of his life.

Tychyna's early collections were the culmination of three decades of Ukrainian literary modernism in both the Russian and Austro-Hungarian empires. In Ukraine, the term 'modernism', applied more narrowly than in English-speaking countries, designates a movement in the arts of the late nineteenth and the early twentieth centuries that foregrounded the autonomy of art and art's vocation to create objects of beauty. Embracing tendencies that have also been called Neo-Romanticism, Symbolism, *décadence*, Art Nouveau and *fin de siècle*, East European modernists generally de-emphasised the role of art in representing or seeking to change social life and distanced themselves from exponents of realism, for whom the social role of the arts was paramount.

The modernist movement in Ukrainian literature of the early twentieth century comprised a small number of major figures – Olha Kobylianska, Lesia Ukrainka, Mykhailo Kotsiubynsky, Vasyl Stefanyk and Volodymyr Vynnychenko – and a lively collection of other poets, writers and critics who gravitated toward particular groupings or journals. In Lviv, several writers came together in 1906 to form a group called the Young Muse. In the Russian Empire, the liberalisation following the revolution of 1905 eased conditions for Ukrainian-language publishing, enabling the establishment in 1909 of the journal *Ukrainska khata* (Ukrainian House) as a venue for the publication of modernist authors.

Modernism became a topic of heated debate within the literary community. The antimodernist flagbearer was the literary critic Serhii Yefremov (1876–1939), whose essay 'In Quest of a New Beauty' (1902) castigated modernists for artistic weakness, lack of social engagement and even depravity. Yefremov was especially scathing in his attack on Olha Kobylianska, whose work modernists admired. Ivan Franko, the pre-eminent literary and intellectual authority of Western Ukraine, was sarcastically dismissive of the Young Muse poets, even though his own collection *Ziviale lystia* (Withered Leaves, 1896) could be seen to fit within their aesthetic paradigm. At the heart of the issue was a divide between proponents of a view of literature as means for the betterment of the nation at large and its majority, the ordinary people, and advocates for the creation of a national high culture capable of appealing to an intellectual audience on par with the high cultures of other European nations. In fact, both sides strove for the one goal: a literature serving the best interests of Ukraine as they understood them.

There was a great deal of stylistic and thematic coherence in the poetry produced by Ukrainian modernists in both empires. At its best, their poetry is mellifluous, its control of verse forms refined. Melancholy is a prevailing tone, as in 'Gilded Sorrow' (*100Y*: 111) by Vasyl Pachovsky (1878–1942), and solitude is a frequent theme, as in 'Alone Again, Again Alone' (*UP*: 281) by Mykola Filiansky (1873–1938). Objects of the natural world are often evocatively described as embodiments of beauty, where beauty is no mere attribute but a thing in itself. Such are the poems 'In the Embraces of Grapevines White Lilacs have Fallen Asleep' (*100Y*: 105) and 'Early Spring' (*UP*: 295) by, respectively, Petro Karmansky (1878–1956) and Hryhorii Chuprynka (1879–1921). A structural device often encountered is the analogy: in 'A Palimpsest' (*UP*: 297) by Mykola Vorony (1871–1942), a text, presumably sacred, by St John fades to reveal an erased work, presumably scurrilous, by the satirist Aristophanes. This re-emergence is then compared to the reawakening within the lyrical subject of a long-extinct love.

Social motifs are not wholly foreign to the modernists, even if, in 'Harvest Time' (*UP*: 278–9) by Mykola Cherniavsky (1868–1938), the sight of labouring villagers inspires, not outrage at social injustice, but aesthetic contemplation. Filiansky's 'The Mother' (*UP*: 291), on the other hand, is a cry for sympathy with the woman exhausted and ultimately done to death by 'work, endless work'. The poetry of Bohdan Lepky (1872–1941) shares the melancholy mood of much Ukrainian modernist poetry. A proportion of his verse expresses patriotic sentiment grounded in history: in 'The Village Comes From Days Long Lost', a group of villagers singing 'an ancient song' causes the lyrical subject to reflect on his people's past military glory and to hope for its return (*UP*: 304–5). Ahatanhel Krymsky (1871–1942) was a noted scholar of the Orient whose travels in the Middle East inspired such poems as 'I Climbed the Crest . . .' (*UP*: 270–71). Melancholy, yearning for an inaccessible beloved, and a pantheistic perception of nature characterise Krymsky's poetry; the fusion of spirit and body, of sacredness and bodily delight are the themes, for example, of 'The Prophet Speaks: "I Like to Pray . . ."' and 'You'll Lose the Custom of Thinking' (both *100Y*: 99).

Like Ukrainian modernist poets, their colleagues working in prose aspired to, and often achieved, a high degree of artistry in their compositions, especially in the short genres. Economical, well-crafted plots and skilfully controlled tension characterise many such works, as do urban settings and the depiction of the Ukrainian populace as socially and ethnically diverse. It was in their prose works that Ukrainian modernists joined their colleagues in the rest of Europe in addressing topical intellectual issues. The importance, and at the same time the mysteriousness, of sexual drives is the motor of many plots, including those of 'The She-Devil' (*RH*: 168–85) by Hnat Khotkevych (1877–1938) and of Kotsiubynsky's story 'The Debut' (1909, *RH*: 186–215). In the latter, a young man obsessed with a woman he considers unattractive cannot decide whether his emotion is love or hate. The unfettered pursuit of self-fulfilment by powerful individuals in the spirit of Nietzsche's *Übermensch* is the theme of a number of stories where, reversing the conventional hierarchy, a weak man yields to a strong, sexually uninhibited woman. Among such works are Cherniavsky's 'The End of the Game' (1901, *RH*: 11–21) and Khotkevych's 'The Prodigal Son' (1898, *RH*: 138–67), as well as Vynnychenko's 'The Clandestine Affair' (*RH*: 325–39) and 'The Chain' (*PBC*: 259–73).

Ukrainian modernists associated the motif of the charismatic, sexually potent and socially powerful man, not with contemporary urban environments, but with exotic places where, in their view, the primeval biological nature of human beings had not yet been blunted by civilisation. The Carpathian Mountains were such a setting, and they fascinated Ukrainian modernists. Kotsiubynsky, Khotkevych and Lesia Ukrainka all visited the Carpathians; Kobylianska lived nearby. The mountains were the homeland of the Hutsuls, a branch of the Ukrainian people imagined as untouched by modernisation. Their culture of everyday life was rich in ritual, their clothes archaic and colourful and their sexual mores surprisingly unfettered even for liberal-minded *fin-de-siècle* intellectuals. The Hutsuls provided unparalleled material for modernist explorations of instincts as drivers of human action. The Carpathians are the setting of Khotkevych's *Kaminna dusha* (The Stone Soul, 1911), Kotsiubynsky's *Shadows of Forgotten Ancestors* (1912, 1981), the literary source for Parajanov's film, and three remarkable prose works by Kobylianska: *Nature* (1895, 2000), 'The Free-Spirited Woman' (1896, *BLS*: 82–121) and *On Sunday Morning She Gathered Herbs* (1909, 2001).

Olha Kobylianska (1863–1942; Figure 7 shows her with her friend and fellow writer Lesia Ukrainka) lived in the Austro-Hungarian province of Bukovyna, whose northern half was peopled mainly by Ukrainians, while Romanians were the majority in the south; there was also a large Jewish minority. The socially and culturally dominant language in the neighbouring province of Galicia, in whose eastern half Ukrainians were the majority population, was Polish; in Bukovyna, German was the language of prestige. It was the language in which Kobylianska encountered European high culture and composed her early, to this day unpublished, works.

Kobylianska's debut novel *A Human Being* (1894, *FCB*: 160–218) established her as a serious intellectual voice in the new Ukrainian literature. The

Figure 7 Olha Kobylianska (left) and Lesia Ukrainka, 1901.
Public domain image.

novel's plot develops a feminist argument about the injustice of a society where a middle-class woman, should she happen to be poor, cannot support herself independently and must marry, even if she feels no affinity with her marriage partner. Kobylianska had acquainted herself with the tenets of Darwinism, and *A Human Being* illustrates a Darwinist thesis: the heroine's marriage to an unloved but virile man who is physically and socially powerful has a logic that is biological, if not cultural. The biological theme is developed more explicitly in the novella *Nature*, published the following year, where the indulged daughter of a city lawyer and a physically attractive Hutsul man have a sexual encounter that both desire. Socially transgressive, the act is rendered inevitable by the physical demands of human 'nature'.

Kobylianska's engagement with the writings of Friedrich Nietzsche gave rise to the satirical 'humoresque' 'He and She' (1895, *BLS*: 12–36), which mocks young intellectuals who quote Nietzsche while remaining unaware of their innate philistinism, and the novel *Tsarivna* (Princess, 1896), where the central character, a woman, aspires to become a Nietzschean free spirit, open to the self-refinement and self-elevation that are hallmarks of the *Übermensch*. In 1902, Kobylianska's *Zemlia* (Land) was published. Generally read as the story of a fratricide resulting from a struggle between two peasant brothers over the right to inherit the patrimonial farm, the novel is, like *Princess*, a demonstration of the unknowable and unpredictable in human affairs.

Princess, *Land* and the other novels that Kobylianska wrote in the decades following have not been translated into English, unlike many of her short works (see *BLS*: 4–335; *WCS*: 256–301; *FCB*: 219–309). The latter include psychological sketches, stories illustrating social hardship and injustice, a remarkable portrayal of the nature-destroying industrial logging of a primeval forest ('The Battle', 1896; *BLS*: 57–77), word-pictures of beautiful objects that emulate in prose the elegance of art nouveau decorative art, and *Valse Mélancolique* (1897, *BLS*: 128–70), a portrait of three young women of contrasting character and world view who share an apartment. There are also later narratives about the horrors of the First World War.

In 1901, the poet and dramatist Lesia Ukrainka visited Kobylianska in Bukovyna. They developed a close friendship; their correspondence is couched in affectionate terms in which some scholars have seen a homoerotic dimension. Lesia Ukrainka (pseudonym of Larysa Kosach, 1871–1913) is, alongside Shevchenko and Ivan Franko, one of the triptych of writers celebrated as builders of the cultural, and by extension political, Ukrainian nation. Larysa Kosach was born into a relatively well-to-do intellectual family. Her mother was a feminist activist and a writer (she published under the pseudonym of Olena Pchilka). Her uncle, the political theorist Mykhailo Drahomanov, advocated for socialism and Ukrainian autonomy within the Russian Empire. She read widely; intellectualism characterises all of her work. As a teenager, Lesia Ukrainka contracted tuberculosis of the bone, a fact that left its mark on the remainder of her life, a great part of which was spent in travels through Europe and, in later life, to Egypt for medical treatment or climate cures.

The struggle to prevail against illness becomes, in Lesia Ukrainka's early poetry and, most famously, in 'Contra spem spero' (I Hope Against Hope, dated 1890), an allegory of the nation's struggle to flourish despite adversity. Equally reflective of the motif of overcoming obstacles is the structure of her poetry: it adheres strictly to classical forms, including difficult ones. Lesia Ukrainka wrote some of her most original poetry, where lyrical contemplation of the surrounding world accompanies philosophical reflection and self-analysis, in British-occupied Egypt. The cycle 'Spring in Egypt', composed in 1910, turns observation of the desert, the desert wind and the people of the Nile valley into an acknowledgment of the poet's collusion, despite humanitarian intentions, in the European colonial project (excerpted in Ukrainka 1975: 125–33).

Lesia Ukrainka also authored works of imaginative prose, literary criticism, and cultural and political polemic. But it was in the genres of drama and the dramatic poem that she most fully expressed her thought-world. Lesia Ukrainka found the dialogue form well suited to articulating diverse perspectives on complex questions. In order to keep such intellectual experiments free of direct (as distinct from allegorical) reference to contemporary social and political issues, she usually set her dramas in such historically and geographically remote places as the ancient Mediterranean basin, the Old Testament Middle East, early Christian communities or seventeenth-century Massachusetts. Her mastery of blank verse enabled her to balance between the distancing sonority of high style and the naturalness of ordinary speech. Only her first drama, *Blakytna troianda* (The Blue Rose, 1908; dated 1896), was in prose; only it was set in a contemporary urban middle-class milieu; only it treated such topical psycho-logical issues as hysteria and genetically inherited mental illness.

Lesia Ukrainka was acutely aware of the oppression imposed by autocracy and colonialism; the quest for freedom from within a condition of unfreedom is the theme of several of her dramas. *In the Catacombs* (1906, 1971) asks about the extent to which spiritual freedom can compensate for the lack of social freedom. *In the Babylonian Captivity* (written in 1902–05; 1908, *SF*: 92–111) and *The Orgy* (1913, *LU*: 143–80) pose the question of whether an artist who survives by serving the oppressor is guilty of betrayal. *In the Wilderness* (written in 1897–1909; 1910, *AMUD*: 7–65), set in the time of Puritan theocracy in New England, argues that flight from one form of unfreedom (in this case, religious) may plunge the artist into a situation even more inimical to creativity, such as a society where the pursuit of wealth produces indifference to art. In *Martianus the Advocate* (1911, *SF*: 261–320), early Christian charity is endangered by the restrictive regulations of ecclesiastical authority. Most provocatively, *The Noblewoman* (1914, *SF*: 11–170), set in the seventeenth century, contrasts the relative freedom enjoyed by the heroine as a privileged woman in the Cossack state to the subservience into which she is thrust when she marries a Muscovite boyar and moves to Moscow.

A few plays address quite different questions. *Cassandra* (written in 1901– 07; 1908, 2024) poses, but does not answer, a query topical in our age of social media: what can count as truth? Cassandra's prophesy, which infallibly predicts the future, but which nobody heeds? Or the self-interested inventions of the charlatan Helenus, who prophesies what people wish to hear? In *The Stone Host* (1912, *LU*: 87–142), the Don Juan plot serves as a base for a discussion of the temptations of power: Donna Anna, in relation to whom Don Juan turns out to be a weakling, displays the will to inherit and exercise the patriarchal authority that her father, the Commander, represents. The most popular of Lesia Ukrainka's plays is also the most Neo-Romantic: *The Forest Song* (1912, *IDL*: 315–485). Set in a forest in Volyn (North-Western Ukraine), the dramatist's birthplace, it narrates the unhappy encounter between the human world and the world of folkloric mythical beings. Neither love (between a young villager and a wood nymph) nor art (the music of the young man's flute) can bridge the gulf between nature and modernity.

Drama was one of the many metiers of the mercurial writer and politician Volodymyr Vynnychenko (1880–1951). An activist of several parties of the extreme left, he was a member of the Central Rada and twice headed its General Secretariat. Disagreements with leaders of the Ukrainian People's Republic led to his emigration in 1919; after a brief return and political flirtation with Lenin, he left Ukraine permanently, living in several European countries before finally settling in the south of France in 1934.

Vynnychenko's early short stories won the approval of critics and public alike. The handful that have been translated (Vynnychenko 1991b; 2014) give an idea of their energetic plots: very young people can hardly disentangle dangerous revolutionary activity from the breathless exploration of first love; a sane man feigning madness to avoid military service is driven mad in a lunatic asylum; two Ukrainians are arrested, one because of his hyperbolic and belligerent patriotism, and the other, who has cautiously kept his Ukrainianness to himself, for association with the first. Vynnychenko's stories of the 1900s and 1910s combine plausible representation of the details of life with a touch of satirical irony at the expense of both the characters represented, and the narrator himself.

Alone among Ukrainian writers, Vynnychenko enjoyed success in interwar Europe. Perhaps because of their Ibsen-like sharpness in dramatizing topical issues, Vynnychenko's plays were popular in German and Italian theatres, and in Germany *Black Panther and Polar Bear* (1911, 2020a) was made into a film. The play is shrill and sensational; its main protagonist is a painter whose commitment to his art is so extreme that, given the choice between perfecting his masterpiece and saving his sick child's life, he chooses the former.

Vynnychenko advocated for a code of 'honesty with oneself' – acting according to one's own wishes and beliefs, rather than deferring to tradition or others' opinions. This meant ignoring the restraints of received morality, especially in sexual matters. The difficulties of adhering to such a code, even for revolutionaries committed to upending the old social order, give rise to dramatic conflicts in such plays as *Disharmony* (1906), *Bazaar* (1910) and *Sin* (1919) (see Vynnychenko 2020b) and the novel *Notes of a Pug-Nosed Mephistopheles* (1917, 2001). In his émigré years, Vynnychenko's thinking about the future took a speculative bent, reflected in his utopian science-fiction novel *Soniachna mashyna* (The Solar Machine, 1928), his play *The Prophet* (1929, *AMUD*: 195–244) about capitalism's seizure of the technology of mass communication and his novel *A New Commandment* (1950, 1991a) with its proposal for a new morality.

The prose of Mykhailo Kotsiubynsky (1864–1913) is conventionally referred to as 'Impressionist'. The label is apt for a handful of his short prose works that recreate in words the imprint that the outside world, mediated through the senses, makes on the consciousness. The crowning example of this technique is the short story 'Intermezzo' (1908, 2017), the first-person inner monologue of an overworked and nervously exhausted city dweller who takes a holiday in the country; the sunlight and shadow, the 'noise of the field', the smell of fresh bread and other wholesome sensory inputs restore his mental equilibrium. In 'Apple Blossoms' (1902, Kotsiubynsky 1973: 106–25), the first-person narrator, a writer, waits in anguish as his young daughter succumbs to a fatal illness, but is unable to switch off the mental mechanism that turns every experience, even the death of his child, into material for future literary works.

Most of Kotsiubynsky's writing, however, is remarkable for creating believable descriptions of psychological states and social phenomena. 'Laughter' (1906, 1973: 69–86) and 'He is coming' (1906, 1973: 87–103) picture the panic that besets, in the first case, the family of an anti-regime intellectual and, in the second, a small-town Jewish community as they await pro-tsarist processions that might turn into pogroms. What was modern about Kotsiubynsky's prose was not so much its form as the social subject matter that it depicted. The agricultural workers in the two short novels that constitute his *Fata morgana* (1903/1910, 1980) are not a nineteenth-century quiescent suffering peasantry, but an agrarian proletariat ripe for revolutionary violence.

In the 1890s, Kotsiubynsky worked for the Odesa Phylloxera Commission, which gave him occasion to travel in grape-growing regions. These contributed settings for stories rich in the local colour of Moldova (e.g., 'Oven Bride', 1896; Kotsiubynsky 1958: 9–34) and Qırım ('On the Rocks', 1902; Kotsiubynsky 1973: 14–36). Exoticism was also a feature of the short novel *Shadows of Forgotten Ancestors* (1911, 1981). Set in the Carpathians, the tale romantically combined passionate love, ancient feuds, jealousy, violence and death with depictions of folkloric ritual and superstition.

Among the period's most powerful, affecting and innovative prose writers, Vasyl Stefanyk (1871–1936) was born into a prosperous peasant family in Western Ukraine. He found his metier in short-form prose on a single theme: the harsh life and resultant psychological suffering of the peasantry of his native Pokuttia region. These miseries, channelled through the consciousness of his tormented characters and all the more convincing for being expressed in language bearing the marks of the Pokuttia dialect, become symbolic of the anguish and helplessness that in Stefanyk's vision characterise the human condition. Later readers have observed affinities between Stefanyk's world view and the sensibility of the Existentialist movement. Stefanyk's creative output was small. *Synia knyzhechka* (The Blue Book, 1899), which won immediate acclaim, and three other collections appeared before 1905. A long hiatus preceded his final collection, *Zemlia* (Earth, 1926). Politically active in the interests of his rural constituents, Stefanyk represented them in the Austrian parliament for the decade preceding the fall of the Habsburg Empire. Among Stefanyk's most admired stories are 'A Stone Cross' and 'Sons' (respectively, 1899 and 1922; Struk 1973: 145–54 and 158–62; for a representative selection of the author's prose, see Stefanyk 1971).

The years 1917 and 1918 were important for two other ethnocultural groups on the territory of today's Ukraine: supporters of a modern Yiddish-language-based culture for Jews on the territory of the former empire, and Crimean Tatars. In September 1917, the Central Rada convened in Kyiv a Congress of Enslaved Peoples of Russia. The Congress was attended by representatives of Crimean Tatars, including Noman Çelebicihan (1885–1918), author of the poem that has become the Crimean Tatars' national hymn and leader of the activists who in December that year created a Crimean national assembly, the Qurultay. Literature, notably the poetry of Hasan Çergeyev (1879–1946) and Üsein Şâmil Toktargazy (1881–1913), like the journalism of İsmail bey Gaspıralı (Ismail Gasprinsky, 1851–1914), had played its part in awakening the Crimean Tatar national consciousness of which the creation of the Qurultay was an expression (Finnin 2022: 54–71).

In January 1918, the Ukrainian People's Republic passed a law introducing 'national-personal autonomy' – an arrangement under which national minorities would be funded by the state to run their own cultural affairs through elective bodies. The law did not outlast the Republic, but was in force long enough for the Yiddish Kultur-Lige, an organisation committed to building for Jews a modern Yiddish-language high culture, to be established in Kyiv. It remained active until 1922. Among those involved in its work were the prose writer and essayist David Bergelson (1884–1952), the poets Dovid Hofshteyn (1889–1952) and Leib Kvitko (1890–1952) and the poet and playwright Peretz Markish (1895–1952). All four were executed in Moscow in 1952 in the Night of the Murdered Poets. Women poets writing in Yiddish in Ukraine at the time included Dina Lipkis (1900–?), Khane Levin (1900–69), Shifre Kholodenko (1909–74) and Aniuta Piatigorskaia (1893–1943) (Burstin 2020). The best known Yiddish writers of the preceding generation who were active in Ukraine were Mendele Mocher Sforim (pseudonym of Sholem Yankev Abramovich, 1836–1917), considered a progenitor of modern Yiddish literature, and Sholem Aleichem (pseudonym of Solomon Rabinovich, 1859–1916), author of *Tevye the Dairyman* (1894; several English translations are available), the literary source for the musical *Fiddler on the Roof* (1964).

1876: Empires Endured

On 13 May 1876, holidaying in the German health spa Bad Ems, tsar Alexander II approved the Ems Decree, which forbade the publication of original works and translations in Ukrainian (except for historical documents and literary works), the import into the Russian Empire of Ukrainian-language materials from abroad as well as stage performances and public readings in Ukrainian. The Ems Decree was not the first such document: in 1863, the minister for internal affairs Petr Valuev instructed Russia's censorship authorities not to allow the publication of Ukrainian-language religious books or school textbooks. The measures were designed to forestall the development, through education, of a cultural identity among the majority population that might evolve into a national consciousness favourable to separatism. In theory, literary texts were excluded from the prohibitions. In practice, censors and writers alike understood that any writing in Ukrainian was suspect. The effects were palpable. During the 1860s and 1870s, years during which the European realist novel flourished, Ukrainian literature languished.

The years preceding the Valuev Circular had been promising. Ukrainian prose, which had struggled to shed its sentimental and self-parodic tone, was reinvented as a medium for socially critical literature by Marko Vovchok (pseudonym of Maria Markovych, née Vilinskaia, 1833–1907). A Russian, she mastered Ukrainian as spoken by ordinary people in the course of her folkloric research. Her collection *Ukrainian Folk Stories* (1857, 1983b) was enthusiastically received. Vovchok imparted to her first-person narrators the voices of peasant women; her depiction of the physical and mental abuse that peasants, especially women, suffered under serfdom resonated with public opinion in the Russian Empire on the eve of the emancipation of the serfs in 1861. The short novel *After Finishing School* (1862, 1983a) paints an almost grotesque portrait of a graduate of an elite girls' school who grows into a psychopathic abuser of serfs and members of her own family alike. Vovchok's story *Maroussia* (1871, 1890), addressed to a young readership, tells of a teenage girl who undertakes a dangerous mission to help Cossacks in their struggle for freedom. Probably written in Russian, the work became popular throughout Europe through a French-language adaptation; a translation published in the United States, with no attribution to Vovchok, was the first Ukrainian literary work to appear in English. Marko Vovchok also authored several novels in Russian, which, however, enjoyed little success.

Marko Vovchok is generally viewed as an early Ukrainian representative of 'Realism' – a combination of intellectual stance and literary style whose features include close attention to the workings of human societies, the attribution of psychological or social causes to the behaviour of human individuals and, very often, criticism of prevailing social relations. Realism was, in Ukraine as elsewhere in Europe, the dominant literary mode of the last third of the nineteenth century. In the Russian Empire, however, restrictions on Ukrainian-language publications together with the underdevelopment of a market for literature in Ukrainian resulted in very few authors donning the mantle of novelist. Anatolii Svydnytsky (1834–71) completed *Liuboratski*, a novel about a clerical family, in the early 1860s, but it was published only in 1886, in Lviv.

The displacement of Ukrainian publishing activity from the Russian Empire to Lviv was one of the consequences of the Valuev Circular and the Ems Decree. Links between Ukrainian writers and intellectuals in the two empires intensified, as did their sense of belonging to a single cultural nation. Almost all the works of the prolific novelist Ivan Nechui-Levytsky (1838–1918) appeared in Lviv – including *Mykola Dzheria* (1880), the narrative of a young villager's travels across Ukrainian landscapes as he endures exploitative work in factories and other workplaces, and *Kaidasheva simia* (Kaidash's Family, 1879), a grotesque depiction of petty conflict within a peasant family. Panas Myrny (1849–1920) and Ivan Bilyk (1845–1905) published their *Khiba revut voly, yak yasla povni?* (Do Oxen Low When Mangers Are Full?) in Geneva in 1880. The first parts of Myrny's *Poviia* (Prostitute, 1883/1884) were, however, able to be published in Kyiv.

Neither Svydnytsky's novel nor those of Nechui-Levytsky or Myrny have been translated into English, although a short excerpt of *Do Oxen Low* is available (*WBL*: 7–14). Ukrainian realist prose is represented in English by short-form works, many in the translations of Roma Franko (*BLS, FCB, IDN, ST* and *WCS*). Women figure prominently as authors of these stories: those who wrote in the Russian Empire include Olena Pchilka (pseudonym of Olha Kosach, 1849–1930), Hrytsko Hryhorenko (pseudonym of Oleksandra Sudovshchykova-Kosach, 1849–1930), Liubov Yanovska (1861–1933) and Dniprova Chayka (pseudonym of Liudmyla Vasylevska, 1861–1927), and in the Habsburg lands Nataliia Kobrynska (1855–1920) and Yevheniia Yaroshynska (1868–1904). Pchilka and Kobrynska were leaders of early Ukrainian feminism; to a greater or lesser degree, all six authors viewed social realities through a feminist lens. Also of note as examples of the realist mode are the short stories of Stepan Vasylchenko (1878–1932) (*WBL, RH*).

The prohibitions of 1863 and 1876 dealt a heavy blow to the publication of Ukrainian poetry in the Russian Empire. Yakiv Shchoholiv (1923–98) published his first collection in 1843; the next appeared in 1883. The first poetry collection of the fabulist Leonid Hlibov (1827–93) was published in Kyiv in 1863, but most of the print run was destroyed. Stepan Rudansky (1834–73), the author of humorous verse *spivomovky* – 'singspeeches' – was not published in his lifetime. Their poetry, as well as that of Ivan Manzhura (1851–93), Volodymyr Samiilenko (1869–1925), the revolutionary and exile Pavlo Hrabovsky (1864–1902), the theatre activist Mykhailo Starytsky (1840–1904) and the west Ukrainian poets Osyp Makovei, Sydir Vorobkevych (1836–1903) and Yurii Fedkovych (1834–88), is represented in *UP* (159–93, 246–53, 261–8). Social criticism and patriotic commitment characterised the work of all of these poets. Fedkovych, a belated Romantic, served as an officer in the Austro-Hungarian army and wrote a number of powerful poems decrying the lot of the common soldier.

In 1881, the prohibition of Ukrainian-language theatre was relaxed some-what, enabling drama to play a major role in nurturing Ukrainian national identity between the 1880s and the First World War. A number of talented writers – Starytsky, Marko Kropyvnytsky (1840–1910) and Ivan Karpenko-Kary (pseudonym of Ivan Tobilevych, 1845–1907) – created a repertoire of plays that were stage-friendly and enduringly popular, notwithstanding the objections of critics desirous of more sophisticated theatrical fare. None of these dramas, tied as they are to the social specificities of the post-emancipation Ukrainian village (representation in Ukrainian of the educated classes remained forbidden), are available in English.

In Austria-Hungary, the leading Ukrainian literary figure of the last quarter of the nineteenth century and the first decade of the twentieth was Ivan Franko (1856–1916), prolific poet and prose writer, public intellectual and political organiser, critic and historian of literature, folklorist, philologist, translator and editor. A socialist in his youth, he later viewed national liberation as a prerequisite of social emancipation. Franko was born in a village in Western Ukraine not far from the oil-mining town of Boryslav, the setting of many of his early prose works. His father was a prosperous village blacksmith, and his mother the descendant of an impoverished noble family. Franko identified with the working masses, often referring to himself as a 'peasant's son'. At Lviv University, he read socialist theorists, including Ferdinand Lasalle and Friedrich Lange. He was imprisoned three times for his political activities. Franko's Boryslav cycle of short stories (1877–1899) and the novel *Boryslav in Flames* (1881/1882, 2023a) vividly illustrated the Marxist conception of class struggle: they showed capitalist mine owners mercilessly exploiting oil industry workers and anticipated worker resistance in the form of consciousness-raising, unionisation and disciplined strikes.

This was the period of Franko's programmatic poetry, including 'The Stone-Hewers' (1878) with its allegory of revolutionary intellectuals as manacled slaves cutting a road through rock for the benefit of future generations, and the equally famous 'Hymn' (1882, Franko 1948: 97–8) of the 'eternal revolution-ary'. It was also the time of the no less thesis-driven historical novel *Zakhar Berkut* (1883, *WBL*: 153–319), set in the thirteenth century, when a small community relying on its ingenuity and unity of purpose defeats an invading Mongol army.

Franko's poetry, often arranged in cycles, displays a great variety of forms and moods. The second edition of the collection *Z vershyn i nyzyn* (From Highlands and Lowlands, 1893), for example, contains both tormented lyrics of unrequited love (the cycle 'Ziviale lystia' (Withered Leaves)) and political verse (the cycle 'Dumy proletariia' (Ballads of a Proletarian)). Franko's long narrative poems included *The Master's Jests* (1887, 1979), about the abuses enabled by serfdom, and tales of heroic outsiders: the religious polemicist of the turn of the sixteenth century Ivan Vyshensky (Franko 1983) and, above all, Moses (Franko 1973). Franko, doubtless, personally identified with the prophet driven by unconditional love for his people, and yet exasperated by their sloth and indifference. His most popular work was a verse satire based on the fable of Reynard the Fox, *Fox Mykyta* (1891, 2000). Notwithstanding their somewhat archaic flavour, Percival Cundy's chrono-logically arranged translations give a reliable picture of Franko's poetic oeuvre (Franko 1948).

After the Boryslav narratives, Franko wrote numerous novels and much short-form prose in a realist vein, experimenting from the 1910s onward with elements of modernist style and content. Almost nothing of this large corpus has been translated into English. His best-known dramatic work is the psychological drama *Stolen Happiness* (1893, 2023b).

Among realist authors living in Ukraine but writing in languages other than Ukrainian were the prolific Polish novelist Józef Ignacy Kraszewski (1812–87), several of whose books, including *Jermoła* (1857, 1891), were based on the author's life in Volyn, and the German writer of Jewish background Karl Emil Franzos (1848–1904), author of several novels set in the Jewish or Ukrainian communities of the eastern provinces of Austria-Hungary, including, respectively, *The Jews of Barnow* (1877, 1883) and *For the Right* (1882, 1888). The best-known German-language writer from Ukrainian lands was Lviv-born Leopold von Sacher-Masoch (1836–95), author of *Venus in Furs* (1870, 1921), the Ukrainian part of whose surname is immortalised in the term for the psychosexual disorder.

1847: From People to Nation

On 30 March 1847, the historian Mykola Kostomarov, less than a year into his appointment as an adjunct professor at Kyiv University, was to be married. On 28 March, however, he was arrested on suspicion of seditious activity as a member of a secret society called the Brotherhood of Saints Cyril and Methodius. The same fate befell Kostomarov's friends, Taras Shevchenko, a painter and already a poet of renown, and the prose writer, poet and cultural activist Panteleimon Kulish. Brought to Saint Petersburg, they were imprisoned, interrogated and sentenced to punishments of varying levels of severity. There was no legal process. Shevchenko's sentence was the harshest: banishment as a common soldier to outposts in the depths of the empire. The tsar added in his own hand a prohibition on painting and writing. Kostomarov, exiled to the city of Saratov on the Volga, got off relatively lightly. Decades later, he described the ordeal in two autobiographies (*FMU*: 38–47, 93–100).

The Brotherhood of Saints Cyril and Methodius was a small group of young intellectuals who cherished the ideals of personal liberty and the freedom of nations, viewing both as proceeding from the tenets of the Christian faith. Their world view was in harmony with the anti-monarchical national liberalism that in 1848 would find expression in European revolutions from Paris to Budapest (but not in the Russian Empire). The Cyrillo-Methodians were in sympathy with the pan-Slav movement initiated by Slovak, Czech and Serbian intellectuals earlier in the nineteenth century; their visionary objective was a free federation of Slavic republics. Kostomarov, the intellectual leader of the Brotherhood, formulated its ideology in a treatise conventionally called *The Books of Genesis of the Ukrainian People*. It existed in a few manuscript copies and was not published until 1918. Written in a simple but lofty biblical style, the *Books* ascribed to Ukraine a special role among the Slavic nations. Citing Cossack traditions of equality and elective governance and, in Ukrainian society, Christian piety and respect within the family and among the genders, the *Books* prophesied for Ukraine the role of exemplar for all peoples (*TIHU*: 94–100).

Mykola Kostomarov (1817–85) was the son of a Russian aristocrat and a Ukrainian peasant woman. During his studies at Kharkiv University, he became interested in Ukrainian folklore and began his lifelong identification with the Ukrainian people. Kharkiv was the first focal point of Ukrainian Romanticism, whose pre-eminent feature was fascination with the culture and creativity – the 'Spirit' – of the ordinary people. Between 1830 and 1841, a number of almanacs published mainly in Kharkiv contained folkloric texts as well as original compositions in Ukrainian. Izmail Sreznevsky, later an eminent philologist, published several folkloric collections titled *Zaporozhskaia starina* (Zaporozhian Antiquity, 1833/1838; the *Zaporozhtsi* were Cossacks who had been active in the steppes *za Porohamy*, 'beyond the Dnipro rapids'). These collections contained both real and counterfeit examples of the folk historical epics known as *dumy*. A major influence upon the Kharkiv milieu, including Kostomarov, was the folksong collection first published by Mykhailo Maksymovych (1804–37) in 1827.

The poets of the Kharkiv School included Amvrosii Metlynsky (1814–70), Levko Borovykovsky (1806–89) and Mykhailo Petrenko (1817–62), whose folk-influenced, often melancholy poetry on history, especially that of the Cossacks, and nature, especially in its tempestuous moods, is minimally represented in *Ukrainian Poets* (*UP*: 62–74). Kostomarov began writing poetry in Ukrainian as part of a personal mission to increase the amplitude of Ukrainian literature by composing works of 'high' genres, including the philosophical lyric of which his poem 'Hellas' (*UP*: 71) is an example. With this aim in view, he also composed a historical prose drama and a tragedy in verse.

After his arrest, Kostomarov abandoned writing in the Ukrainian language. Nonetheless, many of his voluminous historical works published between the mid-1850s and 1880s dealt with themes from Ukrainian history, mainly of the Cossack period. Kostomarov's historical writings were widely read: his study of Bohdan Khmelnytsky, the Ukrainian military leader who established an independent Cossack state in the mid-seventeenth century, sustained four editions during his lifetime. Kostomarov also wrote four historical novels, which, though set for the most part in Russia, included Ukrainian characters illustrative of the freedom-loving disposition, which he regarded as the essence of the

Ukrainian national character. Kostomarov set out his views on the contrasting nature of Ukrainians and Russians in his treatise 'Two Rus' Nationalities' (1861, *FMU*: 134–74), attributing individualism and distaste for authority to the former, communality and a readiness to accept autocracy to the latter.

Panteleimon Kulish (1819–97), like a great many educated Ukrainians of the mid-nineteenth century, was descended from the Cossack elite, most of whom had acquired gentry status in the Russian Empire. His early works included short folklore-inspired stories, a historical novel in Russian and a long historical poem, *Ukraina* (1843), which narrated the history of Ukraine from the Kyivan princes onward as a series of *dumy*. Apart from a few poems (*UP*: 153–85), Kulish's oeuvre is represented in English by his historical novel *The Black Council* (1857, 1973), which he completed in the mid-1840s. Following the template established for the genre by Sir Walter Scott in the 1810s, Kulish embedded a fictional plot within a framework of real historical events, which he meticulously researched. *The Black Council*, set during the struggles for primacy among the Cossacks after the death of Khmelnytsky, did not share Kostomarov's enthusiasm for the Cossacks' democratic spirit, decrying it instead as anarchic, easily influenced by demagoguery and intolerant of prudent leadership. In the epilogue to his Russian version of the novel (*TIHU*: 105–21), Kulish reviewed the linguistic alternatives open to Ukrainian writers. They could publish in Russian, as did Mykola Hohol, familiar in English as Nikolai Gogol, or write for a small readership in a literary language still in formation, but have the satisfaction of articulating the 'thoughts, feelings and movements of the soul . . . which cannot be expressed in a language not native to the author' (*TIHU*: 120).

Hohol (1809–52), also a descendant of Cossack gentry, had famously created engaging sketches of the Ukrainian village and Ukrainian agrarian gentry-folk, as well as uncanny tales reminiscent of motifs in Ukrainian folklore in the collections *Evenings on a Farm near Dikanka* (1831/1832) and *Mirgorod* (1835). The latter contained the Cossack romance 'Taras Bulba', about whose historical plausibility Kulish was less than complimentary. Hohol went on to write his tales of St Petersburg and the satire *Dead Souls* (1842) and became one of the most lauded figures of Russian literature. He has long been the object of divergent judgements by Ukrainian critics. Some have admired the aesthetic flair of his Ukrainian tales and remarked on their capacity to generate emotions of affinity with the country and people they depict. Others have seen him as an implement of the empire whose talent did much to ingrain the idea of Ukraine as a picturesque but peripheral part of a Russian cultural and political whole. Recent studies have highlighted the ambivalence and complexity of his identity and legacy.

As well as a writer, Kulish was an ethnographer, translator and inspirer of literary life. He published a much admired two-volume collection of ethnographic and historical materials, *Zapiski o yuzhnoi Rusi* (Notes on South Rus', 1856/1857); he edited and saw to the publication of Marko Vovchok's *Folk Stories*; he translated the Bible, most of Shakespeare's plays and many other works of European literature; and he was one of the authoritative figures, together with Kostomarov and Shevchenko, behind the publication in 1861–62 of the Ukrainian-themed St Petersburg journal *Osnova* (The Foundation). In the 1870s, however, his negative attitude toward Cossack and peasants revolutions, in parallel with his belief in the beneficence for Ukraine of Russian statehood and Polish aristocratic culture, estranged him from many participants in the Ukrainian movement.

Among other infrequently translated Ukrainian Romantic writers in the Russian Empire were Yevhen Hrebinka (1812–48), remembered mainly as a friend of Shevchenko and the author of verse fables such as 'Ursine Justice' (*UP*: 60–1), the poet Oleksandr Afanasiev-Chuzhbynsky (1817–75), author of a fine verse portrait of the steppe as a phenomenon of natural beauty saturated with the irrecoverable history of the Cossacks (*UP*: 72–3), the poet Viktor Zabila (1808–69) with his poetry of unrequited love, and Oleksa Storozhenko (1805–74), a prose writer and author of the belatedly Romantic gothic verse narrative *Marko Prokliaty* (Marko the Cursed, 1870/1879), a Ukrainian version of the motif of the Wandering Jew.

A Ukrainian Romantic movement emerged across the border in Austria-Hungary, where, in contrast to the Russian Empire, the Ukrainian culture-carrying social group was the clergy. Three Lviv seminarians, Markiian Shashkevych (1811–43), Ivan Vahylevych (1811–66) and Yakiv Holovatsky (1814–88), formed a group that called itself the Rus' Triad. They shared the Romantic preoccupations of their Kharkiv counterparts, collecting folklore, studying Ukrainian history, translating works from other Slavic traditions and writing poetry of their own. They published *Rusalka Dnistrovaia* (The Nymph of the Dnister, 1837), an almanac containing their poems in vernacular Ukrainian, folkloric texts, old lyrical and heroic verse, and translations from Serbian folk poetry. Only a few hundred copies of the almanac, published in Budapest, were distributed; the remainder was intercepted by the authorities. The Triad's poetic output was not large. All three composed poetry on historical and folkloric themes, love poetry and nature lyrics. Shashkevych's nature poems, in particular, are affecting in their simplicity and melancholy tone ('To a Primrose', *UP*: 78). Shashkevych and Holovatsky are represented by a few translations in *UP*, as is a poet of the same period and similar temperament, Mykola Ustyianovych (1811–85) (*UP*: 78–86).

Ukrainian Romantic poets and writers other than Shevchenko had the misfortune of being Shevchenko's contemporaries. From the moment of the publication of Shevchenko's *Kobzar* (The Minstrel) in 1840, their efforts were cast into deep shadow by the radiance of a poet of an altogether different order of magnitude. Dmytro Chyzhevsky, the historian of literature most attuned to language and style as factors that make verse poetic, identified some of the features that give Shevchenko's poetry its musicality and force. Among them are its freedom in the treatment of both folk and classical rhythms, the originality of its aural 'instrumentation' through internal and imperfect rhyme, its sonorous repetitions of sounds and words, its balance between folk, neutral and elevated diction and its avoidance of the appearance of artifice (Chyzhevsky 1997: 498–525). The uniqueness of Shevchenko lay in his capacity to create a poetic language that, for Ukrainians, possessed the quality of naturalness to the point of inevitability, and with this idiom to conjure forth the idea of Ukraine as a collective human entity awaiting realisation in dignity and freedom. With the appearance of Shevchenko's poetry, it became impossible to regard Ukrainian literature otherwise than as the foundation of a project for national liberation.

The significance of Shevchenko's poetry was amplified by the symbolism inherent in his biography. Taras Shevchenko (1814–61; see Figures 8 and 9) was born a serf, bereft of rights, legally the property of his landowning master along

Figure 8 Taras Shevchenko, self-portrait, 1840. Public domain image.

Figure 9 War-damaged monument to Taras Shevchenko, Borodianka near Kyiv, 2022. Photo: State Emergency Service of Ukraine. Reproduced under the Creative Commons Attribution 4.0 International Licence.

with 18,000 others, in a village in the heartland of Cossack Ukraine. His talents at drawing were noticed when he was brought into the estate house as a servant; apprenticed to a painter in St Petersburg, where he went as part of his master's entourage, Shevchenko used the northern capital's 'white' summer nights to sketch the statues in one of the city's parks. Here he was discovered by a member of the St Petersburg Ukrainian community. Welcomed into its circle, he was introduced to such figures of the Russian establishment as the painter Karl Briullov and the poet Vasilii Zhukovsky. Briullov painted Zhukovsky's portrait, which was offered as a prize at a lottery held in the imperial court; the proceeds purchased Shevchenko's freedom and enabled him to enrol as a student at the Imperial Academy of Arts. Meanwhile, he had begun writing and publishing poetry.

After graduating from the Academy in 1845, Shevchenko joined the Kyiv Archeographic Commission, where his task was to travel through Ukraine, sketching historical monuments and collecting folklore. This employment was terminated by his arrest. Sent into indefinite military exile, he continued both writing and drawing, despite the tsar's express prohibition; he even took part in an expedition to explore the Aral Sea as official artist. In 1850, he was transferred to an outpost on the Caspian Sea in today's Kazakhstan, where conditions were more onerous. Nicholas I died in 1855; endeavours by

Shevchenko's friends to free him finally succeeded, and in 1858 he returned to St Petersburg, where he was treated as a celebrity. He resumed writing poetry, revised the poems he had written in exile and experimented with the art and technology of etching. His death, his funeral in St Petersburg, the transportation of his mortal remains to Ukraine and his reburial in Kaniv in a site overlooking the Dnipro were all occasions for solemn public gatherings and speeches that were also manifestations of solidarity with the Ukrainian cause. His grave soon became a place of pilgrimage.

Kobzar is the name conventionally given today to books containing the whole of Shevchenko's poetic corpus. When first published in 1840, however, the *Kobzar* was a collection of only eight poems. The frontispiece by Shevchenko's friend Vasyl Shternberg showed a *kobzar* – a wandering singer of *dumy*, blind and accompanied by a young boy as a guide, and holding his lute-like *kobza*. A *duma* is a folk genre in which the words are intoned (the delivery is akin to recitative) to the accompaniment of a *kobza* or a many-stringed *bandura*. The word 'duma' is related to 'dumka', a thought or meditation. The first poem in the *Kobzar*, translated as 'O My Thoughts, My Heartfelt Thoughts', established the authorial stance that Shevchenko would maintain in much of his oeuvre: like a *kobzar*, he would articulate in words the visions and memories – the 'thoughts' – that welled up within him, hoping that they would reach and move their addressees. The first poem already contains elements characteristic of much of Shevchenko's poetry: recurrent motifs (the Cossack and his horse, the girl with stereotypical 'dark eyes and black brows'), symbolic landscapes (the steppe, the Dnipro, the cherry orchard and the burial mound known as the *mohyla*, popularly imagined to be the resting place of Cossacks, but in fact much more ancient) and the mood of sorrow and loss.

The first *Kobzar* contained two historical poems celebrating the prowess of the Cossacks, 'Ivan Pidkova' and 'The Night of Taras', and two poems on the anguish of a girl whose Cossack lover has failed to return from his campaigns, one short ('Song: What Use are Coal-Black Brows to Me'), and the other a long Romantic ballad involving supernatural elements ('The Poplar'). There were also two poems about fellow adepts of the poetic word: 'Perebendia', which pays homage to a *kobzar*, and 'To Osnovianenko', which honours Hryhorii Kvitka-Osnovianenko, the most respected living Ukrainian writer of the previous generation. Through these two works, Shevchenko defined himself in relation to the old Ukrainian folk tradition and the new tradition of modern Ukrainian literature. The centre of gravity of the collection was the long narrative poem 'Kateryna'. Kateryna, a young village girl, falls in love with a soldier – a *moskal* (the term is ambiguous: at the time, it was both the popular ethnonym for a Russian, and the generic term for a soldier in the imperial army).

He abandons her; with her infant son, she searches for him and finds him, only to be repudiated. She kills herself; her orphaned son becomes the helper of a *kobzar*. The poem invites allegorical reading of the *moskal* as the colonising Russian state, of Kateryna, the exploited victim, as Ukraine, and of her son, the *kobzar's* guide, as the *kobzar's* legatee, the future carrier of the identity and spirit of his people. Other poems of Shevchenko's appeared in Hrebinka's almanac *Lastivka* (The Swallow, 1840), including the Romantic ballad 'The Bewitched', another tale of the tragic consequences of the Cossack's delayed return to the beloved.

In 1841, Shevchenko published the historical poem *Haidamaky*, a panoramic depiction of the 'Koliivshchyna', a violent popular uprising of 1768 in the Ukrainian lands west of the Dnipro, which at the time were the eastern parts of the Polish-Lithuanian Commonwealth. The narrator's voice in *Haidamaky* adopts a position of pan-Slav moral rectitude, deploring the internecine conflict between 'children of the old Slavs'. But the poem overwhelms this ethical framework, rapidly becoming a horror-stricken depiction of mutual violence between Ukrainians and Poles, and of both against Jews. Soviet critics read the poem as an illustration of just retribution against class-based oppression. It is, more plausibly, a terrifying vision of the darkness in human nature that delving into history can unearth.

Shevchenko's two journeys to and within Ukraine between 1843 and 1847 gave rise to a manuscript that he titled *Try lita* (Three Years). *Three Years* contained Shevchenko's best-known poem, 'My Testament', which called upon the poet's compatriots to rise, rend their chains and create a great family, new and free, and three great political poems that analysed with sarcasm and satirical penetration the tyrannical and colonialist essence of the Russian imperial state. 'The Dream (A Comedy)' frames itself as a drunken hallucination on the part of the speaker. He imagines himself to be overflying a land where his bird's-eye perspective reveals abuses suffered by the powerless and poor and cruel punishments inflicted on political prisoners. In a place uncannily like St Petersburg, he witnesses a grotesque ritual, a stinging allegory of autocracy: as the city's notables line up by rank, a tsar delivers a painful punch to the face of the most senior, who extends the favour to the next in line, and so on until the entire population has received its blows, crying 'Hurrah!' in gratitude. 'The Caucasus' lauded the peoples of the Caucasus Mountains for their resistance against Russia and urged them to fight on, praising the justice of their cause. The poem denounced the empire's hatred of the very idea of its neighbours' free and sovereign existence; it mocked colonialist claims to pursue a civilising and Christianising mission, excoriating imperial 'civilisation' as serfdom, social rapacity and Siberian punishment. 'To the Dead, the Living and the Unborn' addressed the Ukrainian gentry-folk who hosted Shevchenko on their estates during his Ukrainian travels and berated them as mediators of oppression: self-congratulatory descendants of Cossack rebels against injustice, they oppress their compatriots as serfs when they should embrace them as brothers.

Religious themes played an important role in Shevchenko's poetry, especially in later life. Charity and spontaneous faith are held up as positive norms against religious hierarchy, dogma, sectarianism and the hypocritical exploitation of religion for selfish ends. Early Christianity provided settings for 'The Neophytes' and 'Mary' (Shevchenko 1964: 483–500, 514–31); the Old Testament became a source for the critique of autocracy and social oppression ('Tsars' and 'Saul', Shevchenko 1964: 358–69, 548–51) and for the promise of salvation for the downtrodden ('Isaiah Chapter 35: An Imitation' and 'Imitation of Psalm XI', Shevchenko 1964: 507). The period of Shevchenko's imprisonment and exile gave rise to poetry on exilic themes: yearnings for the homeland and recollections of youth spent there ('My Thirteenth Year Was Wearing On', 'Even Till Now I Have this Dream', 'To A. O. Kozachkovsky', Shevchenko 1964: 336–41), loneliness ('Once More the Post Has Brought To Me', 'In Captivity I Count the Days and Nights') and the difficulty of writing in isolation from one's audience ('Come, Let Us Turn Again to Versifying', 'Not for the Folk or Their Acclaim', Shevchenko 1964: 350–51, 389–90).

Shevchenko wrote a historical play, *Nazar Stodolia* (1843, first published in 1862), a handful of poems in Russian and, during his years of exile, nine short novels in Russian, which were not published in his lifetime. His fame rests squarely on his Ukrainian-language poetry.

Much of Ukraine had long been part of the Polish-Lithuanian Commonwealth. Several authors of the Polish Romantic movement were born in Ukraine and regarded it as their homeland. They took the country and its history as subject matter for their works – so much so that they are regarded as a 'Ukrainian School' in Polish literature. Novels by members of the School include *Maria: Powieść ukraińska* (Maria: A Ukrainian Novel, 1825) by Antoni Malczewski (1793–1826) and *Zamek kaniowski* (Kaniv Castle, 1828) by Seweryn Goszczyński (1801–76). Józef Bohdan Zaleski (1802–86) composed Cossackophile Byronic lyrics and narrative poems, while Michał Grabowski (1804–63), a friend of Kulish's, wrote prose works on Ukrainian subject matter, including the uprising of 1768 that was the theme of Shevchenko's *Haidamaky*. Juliusz Słowacki (1809–49), too, dealt with the Koliivshchyna in his drama *Sen srebrny Salomei* (Salome's Silver Dream, 1843), one of his several works on Ukrainian historical events.

Mykola Hohol was not the only Ukrainian who contributed to Russian literature. Vasyl Narizhny (Vasilii Narezhny, 1780–1825), best known for his novel *Rossiiskii Zhil Blaz* (The Russian Gil Blas, 1814), wrote novels on

Ukrainian themes, including *Zaporozhets* (The Zaporozhian, 1824) and *Bursak* (The Seminarist, 1824). Orest Somov (1793–1833) wrote Ukrainian-themed historical and gothic prose, including *The Witches of Kyiv* (1833, 2016). The historian Mykola Markevych (1804–60), in addition to his five-volume *Istoriia Malorossii* (History of Little Russia, 1842–43), ethnographic studies and folkloric compendia, authored a collection of ballads titled *Ukrainskiia melodii* (Ukrainian Melodies, 1831).

Ukrainian themes also interested Russian-language writers not of Ukrainian descent. Episodes of Ukrainian struggles for freedom from foreign rule inspired Kondratii Ryleev (1795–1826), author of the poems *Bogdan Khmelnitskii* (1822), *Voinarovskii* (1825) and *Nalivaiko* (1825). Ryleev was executed for his role in the Decembrist uprising of 1825. Alexander Pushkin (1799–1837), on the other hand, penned the poem *Poltava* (1829), which won the approval of Nicholas I and is seen by many as an apologia for Russian imperialism. Its theme was the battle of Poltava of 1709 and preceding events and intrigues. At Poltava, Peter I defeated Charles XII of Sweden and his ally, the Ukrainian hetman Ivan Mazepa, ending hopes for a restoration of Cossack independence.

One of Pushkin's most famous poems, 'Bakhchisaraiskii fontan' (The Fountain of Bağçasaray, 1824), was analysed in a recent study as a key text in the 'de-Tatarisation' of Qırım in the Russian cultural imagination (Finnin 2022: 29, 33–43).

1798: The New Ukrainian Literature Begins

In 1798, Maksym Parpura published in St Petersburg a manuscript that had been circulating among the Ukrainian educated elite and, doubtless, bringing its readers much pleasure: the first three books of *Eneida*, a travesty of Vergil's *Aeneid*, composed in vernacular Ukrainian by Ivan Kotliarevsky (1769–1838; see Figures 10 and 11). Kotliarevsky had received a theological education and worked as a tutor on gentry estates. At the time of the first publication of *Eneida*, he was an officer in the Russian army. Later, he had charge of a hospice for children of impoverished gentry. He took a lively part in the theatrical life of Poltava, his native city. The full text of his *Eneida* (1842, 2004) was published after his death.

Eneida was the first substantial work published in the Ukrainian language as spoken by ordinary people. It retained the plot of the first-century-BC Latin epic: the flight of Aeneas and his companions from defeated Troy, his adventures along the Mediterranean coast and his founding of Rome. But *Eneida* transformed the Trojans into Zaporozhian Cossacks; Vergil's gods and heroes were reborn as representatives of Ukrainian social types. A wealth of Ukrainian

Figure 10 Monument to Ivan Kotliarevsky, Kyiv, 2008.
Photo: Marko Pavlyshyn.

ethnographic detail was woven into the narrative: folk customs, rituals, super-stitions, cuisine and apparel were vividly described. Kotliarevsky employed a jaunty iambic tetrameter and an invariable ten-line stanza form, exploiting to the full the comic potential of rhyme.

Kotliarevsky framed his *Eneida* as a travesty, paying tribute to the Classicist theory of genres that had currency in Europe from the second half of the seventeenth century onward, but by the end of the eighteenth was something of an anachronism. According to the Classicist schema, 'high' genres such as the tragedy and the epic were the domain of deities and royalty, and therefore of elevated language and style. At the other end of the spectrum, characters of low social status populated the genres of comedy, satire and travesty, and were entitled to use low, even vulgar, style and speak the language of the untutored masses. It was in one of these 'low' genres that Kotliarevsky could accommo-date Ukrainian speech.

Writing in the vernacular was not without precedent in the Ukrainian literary tradition. School dramas performed in the Kyiv Mohyla Academy and other educational institutions in the second half of the seventeenth century and for

Figure 11 Monument to Ivan Kotliarevsky in protective sheath, Kyiv, 2022.
Photo: Natalia Lytvynenko. Reproduced by permission.

much of the eighteenth presented serious religious content in a learned language close to Church Slavonic. This main text was interspersed with interludes known as 'intermedia', where characters from lower social strata belonging to various ethnic groups spoke their vernaculars, or parodied versions of them, to comic effect. In Kotliarevsky's days, Ukrainians in the Russian Empire did write in the 'high' genres, but for this purpose they generally used Russian, which as a literary language was more developed than Ukrainian. Vasyl Kapnist (1758–1823), for example, authored 'Oda na rabstvo' (Ode on Slavery, written in 1783, published in 1806) and a five-act verse comedy, *Yabeda* (The Snitch, 1798).

Kotliarevsky's reference to the classicist system of genres implied that, once a more nuanced literary language had evolved, there would be other stylistic registers in which literary works in Ukrainian could be composed. Before long, in his prose play *Natalka Poltavka* (Natalka of Poltava, 1819), Kotliarevsky himself represented the language of the common people as clear and dignified, in keeping with the wisdom and sound ethical intuition of the people themselves. The play served as the basis for the enduringly popular operetta *Natalka Poltavka* (1889) by Mykola Lysenko (1842–1912).

The last third of the eighteenth century saw the rapid erosion of the autonomy of the Cossack state that Bohdan Khmelnytsky had brought under the suzerainty of the Tsardom of Muscovy in 1654. The office of *hetman* (the elected head of the Cossack army and its territories) was abolished in 1764; the *Sich*, the Zaprozhian Cossack headquarters, was destroyed by Russian troops in 1775; and in 1783 the Cossack host itself was absorbed into the regular Russian army. That same year, serfdom was extended to the Ukrainian lands within the Russian Empire, and Russia annexed the territories of the Khanate of Crimea, which for three and a half centuries had been independent or autonomous under the protectorate of the Ottoman Empire.

The Cossacks ceased to be an active component of Ukrainian life and became a symbol of lost freedom. Members of the Ukrainian gentry who drew their lineage from the Cossack officer class thought of the Cossack period as the source of their rights as a distinct social estate. The influential historical treatise *Istoriia Rusov* (History of the Rus', author and date of composition unknown; excerpted in *TIHU*: 82–7) reflected their identity and world view, as did Semen Divovych's *Talk Between Great Russia and Little Russia* (1762, excerpted in *TIHU*: 69–70), which somewhat optimistically asserted that Ukraine and Russia, being subjects of the same monarch, were equals. What Kotliarevsky had modelled in *Eneida* was the connection between the idea of Cossackdom, stripped of its elite connotations, and the culture of the common people. Effectively, this was a proposal for the identity of a modern Ukrainian nation: its present was constituted by Ukraine's popular masses, whose distinctiveness and cultural depth were attested by their folklore and lifeways; its past was the remembered history of the Cossacks with their ethos of freedom and heroism; and its future was what Kotliarevsky's readers could build upon these promising foundations.

In their enthusiasm for the ordinary people and their culture, *Eneida* and *Natalka Poltavka* were in harmony with the works of early Ukrainian Romanticism. In many respects, however, Kotliarevsky's works were beholden to the world view of the age of Enlightenment. That human beings are equal and share equally in human dignity; that ethical intuitions are spontaneous and universal; that altruism is praiseworthy and selfishness contemptible; that the exercise of reason can establish human relations in which justice and happiness prevail – these ideas form the subtext of Kotliarevsky's works, the satirical

Eneida no less than the sentimental *Natalka Poltavka*. Only a few of the songs from the play have been translated into English (see *UP*: 47–9).

The poetic work of the Kharkiv professor Petro Hulak-Artemovsky (1790–1865) vacillated between Classicist amusement, from the perspective of educated high culture, at the customs and values of the peasantry, and Romantic enthusiasm for those very customs and values. Hulak-Artemovsky's small oeuvre includes skilful retellings, humorous and colloquial to the point of vulgarity, but nonetheless elegant, of the odes of Horace in a Ukrainian rural idiom (e.g., 'To Parkhom', *UP*: 52–3) and fables such as 'The Lord and His Dog' (dated 1818; *UP*: 53–8).

The prose writer Hryhorii Kvitka-Osnovianenko (1778–1843) was an heir to the spirit of Enlightenment in contradictory ways. Some of his works generate humour at the expense of the unenlightened masses. In the witty short story 'Saldatsky patret' (The Soldier's Portrait, 1833) – sadly, unavailable in English – a naïve folk narrator invites the distanced amusement of the implied educated audience. The narrative satirically depicts the servile behaviours that the lifelike painting of a soldier, placed in a village market place, induces among local villagers. At other times, evidently moved by the Christian virtue of charity and the enlightened ideal of social equality, Kvitka-Osnovianenko invites his readership into emotional empathy with his plebeian characters. In the sentimental short novel *Marusia* (1833, 1940), an idealised, morally impeccable village girl falls in love. Her father forbids marriage until her beloved earns the wherewithal to buy himself out of the obligation to serve in the army. The young man's return with the requisite money comes too late: Marusia has died while waiting for him. Despondent, he enters a monastery and soon also dies. While it is difficult for today's readers to warm to the story's hyperbolic emotionalism, it was well received by its contemporaries, including Kulish and Kostomarov. *Marusia* treats ordinary folk as objects, not of irony, but of sympathy; the equal participation of the represented community of ordinary people and the educated reading public in a shared emotional experience previsions the trans-class unity of a national audience.

Among the songs in Kotliarevsky's *Natalka Poltavka* was one that began with two lines of a poem by the poet and religious philosopher Hryhorii Skovoroda (1722–94), 'Every City Has Its Customs and Laws' (Skovoroda 2016b: 57). The quotation acknowledged the special regard that Skovoroda, a thinker in the spirit of European Pietism, enjoyed in the popular Ukrainian imagination. The verses came from a collection of poems, each inspired by a Biblical text, composed between 1753 and 1785 and titled *The Garden of Divine Songs*. The purpose of cultivating this 'garden' was to influence readers to live virtuous lives so as to ensure their salvation in eternity. Skovoroda's poems, didactic fables (Skovoroda 1990) and letters (Skovoroda 2016a) are relatively straightforward in content and style. By contrast, his philosophical dialogues, which examine the question of how to understand oneself and, in doing so, live a life that is both valid in itself and acceptable to God, are complex, rich with opaque symbolism and full of allusions to Biblical and classical texts. In 2022, the year of the 300th anniversary of Skovoroda's birth, the museum dedicated to his memory in the country house where he spent the last four years of life was destroyed in a direct strike by a Russian missile.

The eighteenth and early nineteenth centuries saw significant developments in the religious and secular literature of the large Jewish minority on lands encompassed by the present-day borders of Ukraine. Yaakov Yosef of Polonne (d. 1783; according to other sources 1782 or 1784) was the author of *Toledot Yaakov Yosef* (Message of Yaakov Yosef, 1780), the first published text of Hasidism, the mystical movement within Judaism founded by Baal Shem Tov (1698–1760). This and other works of Yaakov Yosef, as well as books based on the teachings of Baal Shem Tov's successor Dov Ber of Mezhyrich (1704–72), were published in Korets in Volyn and Lviv. In the same period, many of the writers associated with Haskalah, the intellectual movement aligned with the European Enlightenment and dedicated to the ideal of renewal within Judaism, were active in Ukraine or commenced their work there. Menachem Mendel Lefin (1749–1826), born in Sataniv, lived for a time in Berlin, but spent most of his life in Galicia, the Habsburg province whose eastern half was populated mainly by Ukrainians. His most influential text, *Cheshbon HaNefesh* (Moral Accounting, 1808, 1996), argued for moral self-reform. He controversially used vernacular Yiddish, rather than Hebrew, in some of his publications. The poet and grammarian Solomon of Dubno (1738–1813) was born in Volyn and studied in Galicia before moving to Amsterdam and finally settling in Berlin, where most of his works were published. Brody, Lviv and Ternopil were foci of a movement critical of Hasidism known as the Galician Haskalah, of which the prose satirist Yosef Perl (1773–1839) was the leading exponent.

For more than a century prior to the partitions of the Polish-Lithuanian Commonwealth, the Ukrainian-settled lands were divided between the Commonwealth and the Tsardom of Muscovy, which was renamed the Russian Empire in 1721. In the Commonwealth, the politically and culturally dominant group was the nobility. Regardless of their ethnic origins, most members of this elite stratum were Roman Catholic, spoke and wrote Polish, and identified with Polish culture. Part of the literature of the Polish Enlightenment was composed in Ukraine by authors with a sense of regional affiliation with the Ukrainian lands. Ukrainian landscape and historical references are present, for example, in the poetry of the poet

Franciszek Karpiński (1741–1825), who was born in Kolomyia. Stanisław Trembecki (1739–1812), a court poet of the last king of Poland, Stanisław Poniatowski, lived for an extended period in Ukraine. His host, a landholder of the Potocki family, created a grand park (today 'Sofiivka', a major tourist attraction) dedicated to his wife Sophia. Trembecki celebrated the park in a long poem, *Sofiówka w sposobie topograficznym opisana wierszem* (Sofiivka Described in Verse in a Topographical Manner, 1806). The poem reflected on philosophical questions topical in the Age of Enlightenment. Its praise for Catherine II, the Russian monarch during whose reign the Commonwealth had been partitioned, disqualified the work in the eyes of most contemporary Poles. Jan Potocki (1761–1815), a member of another Ukrainian-based branch of the Potocki family, wrote in French the remarkable *Saragossa Manuscript* (1805, 1960, 1967). Set in Spain during the Napoleonic Wars, the work, a collection of dozens of stories connected by an intricate frame narrative and incorporating fantastic, gothic, occult, conspiratorial and erotic elements, as well as philosophical reflections, has been regarded by some as a postmodern novel *ante datum*.

In 1774, as one of the outcomes of the Russo-Turkish War, the Khanate of Crimea ceased to be a protectorate of the Ottoman Empire and became a dependency of the Russian Empire. Its formal annexation by Russia in 1783 was soon followed by the abolition of the Khanate, the emigration of a substantial part of the Crimean Tatar elite to Turkey, and the end of the Crimean Tatar courtly secular literature – poetry, but also historical works – of which the khans had been patrons.

1610: Early Modern Multifariousness

In 1610, Meletii Smotrytsky (1577–1633), a teacher at the Orthodox Brotherhood school in Vilnius, published *Thrēnos, That is, The Lament of the One, Holy, Universal, Apostolic Eastern Church, with an Explanation of the Dogmas of the Faith* (1610, Smotryc′kyj 2005: 1–81). The tract presented a defence of Orthodoxy and remonstrated against the Catholic conversions of many Rus′ (Ukrainian and Belarusian) noble families of the Polish-Lithuanian Commonwealth.

The conflict in the Commonwealth between Orthodoxy and Catholicism, both of the Roman and Byzantine rite, had a long gestation. Within a hundred years of the fall of Orthodox Kyivan Rus′ in the thirteenth century, its western parts, corresponding roughly to present-day Ukraine and Belarus, were absorbed into the Grand Duchy of Lithuania and the Kingdom of Poland. In 1569, Poland and Lithuania, long united dynastically, federated to form the Rzeczpospolita, or Commonwealth, a religiously pluralist state where Poles and Lithuanians were mainly Catholic, and Ukrainians and Belarusians mainly

Orthodox. There was also a large Jewish minority. During the Reformation, Lutheranism and Calvinism gained many converts in the Commonwealth. From the mid-sixteenth century onward, the Roman Catholic Church and especially its Jesuit order made concerted efforts to re-establish the pre-eminence of Roman Catholicism in the Commonwealth, targeting not only converts to Protestantism but also traditional adherents of the Orthodox faith.

Endeavouring to reduce the pressure on the Orthodox to convert and on the Rus' nobility to assimilate to Polish culture, the Commonwealth's Orthodox bishops agreed to recognise the supremacy of the Pope and accept Roman Catholic dogma, while retaining eastern cultural traditions, including the use of the Church Slavonic language in liturgy. The rapprochement was formalised in 1596 in Brest, a city today in Belarus. The Union of Brest, however, was rejected by the leading Orthodox magnate Kostiantyn Ostrozky as well as many Orthodox rank-and-file clergy and believers. The result was a split in the Rus' church between those who remained loyal to Orthodoxy (and, from 1620, were supported by the Cossacks) and those who accepted union with Rome; this 'Uniate' church was the antecedent of today's Ukrainian Greek Catholic and Belarusian Greek Catholic Churches.

The struggle between the Christian West and East among the Rus' of the Commonwealth was illustrated in the biography of Smotrytsky himself. He was educated in Ostrozky's school in Ostrih, the Jesuit academy in Vilnius, and in German Protestant schools, including the universities of Wittenberg and Leipzig. He taught in the Vilnius and Kyiv Orthodox Brotherhood Schools and authored a grammar of Church Slavonic that remained authoritative until the first quarter of the nineteenth century, but wrote his polemical works in Polish. In 1618, he took monastic vows in the Orthodox Church and by 1620 held the office of Orthodox Archbishop of Polatsk, Vitsebsk and Mstsislaŭ. Yet in 1627, he converted to the Uniate Church and the following year tried, unsuccessfully, to persuade an Orthodox synod in Kyiv to join the Union.

The *Thrēnos* was characteristic of the learned, rhetorically sophisticated polemical works written mainly in Polish by high-ranking monks and bishops on both sides of the religious divide. The Uniate *Defence of Church Unity* (1617, 1995) by Lev Krevza (d. 1639) elicited an Orthodox response from Zakhariia Kopystensky (c. 1590–1627), the *Palinodia*, written in 1617–24 (Krevza & Kopystens'kyj: 3–156, 157–911). Illustrative of Orthodox monastic piety of a later period is the autobiography of the monk Paisii Velychkovsky (1722–94) (Velyčkovs'kyj 1989). The powerful polemical works, not available in English, of the Orthodox monk Ivan Vyshensky (c. 1550–after 1621) berated not only his ecclesiastical adversaries, but Western and modern cultural influence more generally.

Little of the rich Rus' seventeenth- and eighteenth-century literature is accessible in English. The ornateness of much of this writing, its erudite reference to works of classical antiquity alongside the sacred texts of Christianity, and its understanding of human life in Christian terms as preparation for eternal salvation qualify it as an integral part of European Baroque culture. During this period, church architecture in a native version of the Baroque style flourished in Ukraine. Kyiv's cityscape received its Baroque accents, evident to this day, through the Baroque restoration of medieval monuments, notably the eleventh-century cathedral of Saint Sophia and the churches of the Monastery of the Caves. Essential for the evolution and dissemination of the Baroque world view and cultural style were schools established by Orthodox brotherhoods to compete with Jesuit educational institutions. The Kyiv Academy, founded in 1632 on the basis of such a brotherhood school, became an educational and publishing centre of significance for the whole of Slavic Orthodoxy.

Much Baroque poetry was religious; secular poetry dealt with erotic themes, praised notable personages and articulated political sentiments. Heraldic verse ingeniously described noble families' coats of arms. Poems of eccentric or playful form – epigrams, palindromes and acrostics among them – abounded; Ivan Velychkovsky (d. 1726) was the most famous creator of such verses. Other poets of the age included the churchmen Kasiian Sakovych (1578–1647), Dmytro Tuptalo (1651–1709) and Stefan Yavorsky (1658–1722), as well as Ivan Mazepa (1639–1709), patron of Baroque church-building and the hetman who attempted to re-establish Cossack independence from Muscovy.

The central role of religion in Baroque culture was reflected in the proliferation of theological treatises (in the Rus' literary language of the period, as well as Latin and Polish), collections of sermons, prose lives of monks of the Caves Monastery and other saints, and school dramas of religious content. *About the Harrowing of Hell* (late seventeenth or early eighteenth century, 1989), an Easter play based on the apocryphal story of Christ's visit to Hell following His resurrection, is available in English.

Historical texts, especially the narratives (conventionally called 'chronicles') of 'Samovydets' (the Eyewitness), Hryhorii Hrabianka (1666–c. 1738) and Samiilo Velychko (1670–1728), concentrated on the history of the Cossack and peasant rebellion against Polish rule led by Bohdan Khmelnytsky in 1648, the subsequent wars and Khmelnytsky's creation of an independent Cossack military state from the Ukrainian-settled south-eastern quarter of the Commonwealth. Used as sources by nineteenth-century historians, the chronicles played a major role in shaping Ukrainian national sentiment during the Romantic period.

The Khmelnytsky era was one of the two major themes of folk *dumy*, the other being the earlier Cossack campaigns against Crimean Tatars and Ottoman Turks (see *Ukrainian Dumy* 1979). Many Jews, Poles and Uniates were victims of Cossack and rebel violence during the Khmelnytsky wars; the suffering of Jews in the course of these events was the subject of *Abyss of Despair* (1653, 1950) by the Jewish historian and scholar Nathan Hannover (d. 1683). The Crimean Tatar poet Can-Muhammed Efendi recounted the participation of the Tatars as allies of Khmelnytsky in the war of 1648–49 (Ocakli 2017: 67–68, 91–92). Polish literature of the Baroque period also treated Cossack subject matter. In *Transakcja wojny chocimskiej* (The Progress of the Khotyn War, written in 1669–72, published in 1850), Wacław Potocki (1621–96) took as his theme the battles of 1621 for the Ottoman fortress of Khotyn between Commonwealth and Cossacks forces, on the one hand, and the Ottoman army, on the other.

1185: The Presence of the Medieval Past

On 12 May 1185, an army led by Ihor Sviatoslavych, prince of the Rus' principality of Novhorod-Siversky in the north of present-day Ukraine, was defeated by a force of Cumans (known as Polovtsi in Rus' sources). The battle took place to the east of the Donets River in a part of Ukraine where fighting is under way as I write this. The Cumans were one of a succession of nomadic peoples from Asia that threatened the eastern and southern steppe frontiers of Kyivan Rus' for most of that polity's existence from the late ninth century to the mid-thirteenth. Ihor's campaign, his defeat, capture by the Cumans, escape and return are narrated in detail in a chronicle called the Hypatian after the monastery in Muscovy where the earliest extant manuscript copy of it was held in the seventeenth century.

The same story is told in an epic poem generally regarded as the most accomplished work of Kyivan Rus' literature, *The Tale of Ihor's Campaign* (*UP*: 3–21). The *Tale* came to light in 1791 when Alexei Musin-Pushkin, the finder of a number of important medieval documents, bought it with other manuscripts from a monastery in Yaroslavl in Russia. The *Tale* was published in 1800; the manuscript perished in the fire that destroyed much of Moscow during Napoleon's occupation of that city in 1812.

The *Tale* embellishes the story with speculation on how the mythical bard Boyan might have told it, speeches by Ihor and the princes of other Rus' principalities, a lament by Ihor's wife Yaroslavna, evocations of natural phenomena that portend the doom of the Rus' host, vivid images of armaments and booty, and symbolic language where animals and celestial bodies personify human actors. The authorial voice reminisces about Rus"'s days of military glory, deplores the discord among Rus' princes and urges them to unite in the struggle to defend 'the land of Rus"'. As a secular epic, the *Tale* stands alone in the corpus of Kyivan Rus' writings: there are no works similar to it in genre. Its uniqueness and the fact of the disappearance of the sole manuscript gave rise to a debate over the *Tale*'s authenticity, which has continued into the twenty-first century.

The *Tale of Ihor's Campaign* tells of a period when Kyivan Rus' was in decline. Like much else about Rus', the origin and meaning of the name 'Rus"' are in dispute. Also a matter of controversy is the relative weight of the contributions to the formation of the Kyivan state of Slavic tribes in Kyiv's vicinity and of Scandinavian warrior-traders who used the River Dnipro as part of their trade route from the Baltic Sea to Byzantium. Kyivan Rus' enjoyed periods of stability during the reigns of a few gifted leaders. Volodymyr (whose name in the chronicle record appears as Volodimer) reigned from 980 to 1015 and introduced Christianity in its eastern, Byzantine, form as the religion of the state in 988. Christianity, and with it literacy and religious culture, came to Kyiv from Constantinople, but through the mediation of books imported mainly from Bulgaria and written in Church Slavonic, a language devised for Byzantine Christian missionary activity among Slavic peoples. The reign of Yaroslav (1019–54) saw the construction of major churches, including St Sophia in Kyiv, the foundation of monasteries, princely sponsorship of the copying and translation of religious and other texts, and the composition of the first original Kyivan writings, notably the renowned *Sermon on Law and Grace* by the first native Metropolitan of Kyiv, Ilarion. In general, however, Kyivan Rus' was bedevilled by internecine wars among members of the princely family for the most senior throne, that of Kyiv.

The writings translated in Kyiv for the purpose of deepening instruction in the Christian faith include the *Izbornyky* (compendia) of 1073 (see Figure 12) and 1076 (for the latter, see *EPKR*: 3–118). Collections of texts on theological, historical, biblical and legal themes, they were translated from Greek sources and copied from a Bulgarian compilation. Sermons constituted an important part of the original literature of Kyivan Rus'. Ilarion's *Sermon* (probably dating from the late 1040s, *SRKR*: 3–29) is a masterly exercise in rhetoric and composition. Its structural principle is an analogy between two contrasts: the Old Testament, in which the relationship between God and human beings is characterised by the sternness of law, is juxtaposed against the New, where God communicates with His people through the medium of divine grace. A parallel contrast is drawn between Rus' before and after Kyiv's Christianisation by Volodymyr, whom the sermon praises alongside his son Yaroslav. Also widely

Figure 12 A page from the *Izbornyk* of 1073. Public domain image.

copied and imitated were the sermons of Kiryla (Cyril), bishop of Turaŭ in present-day Belarus (from c. 1130–40 to c. 1182; see *SRKR*: 55–157). Klym Smoliatych, Metropolitan of Kyiv in 1147–54, authored the *Epistle to Foma*, an exercise in the allegorical reading of Scripture (*SRKR*: 31–53).

Lives of saints, a significant genre in Kyivan Rus′ writing, were represented by a number of texts about Borys and Hlib (*HKR*: 1–32, 97–134), sons of Volodymyr whom their elder brother, Sviatopolk, ordered killed to forestall

their possible claims to the Kyiv throne. Canonised as saints, they were vener-
ated as martyrs and exemplars of the virtues of brotherly love and non-violence.
The *Life of Feodosii* (*HKR*: 33–95), written by a monk named Nestor probably
after 1078 and before 1091, lauds one of the two saints (the other being Antonii)
who founded Kyivan monasticism and established the Kyiv Monastery of the
Caves. Stories, some psychologically complex, about monks of that monastery,
sinful as well as virtuous, are narrated in an exchange of letters between two
churchmen in *The Pateryk of the Kyivan Caves Monastery* (original written
between 1215 and 1230, 1989).

Much of what is known or conjectured about Kyivan Rus' comes from
chronicles. Under entries for particular years, in addition to accounts of the
deeds of prices, the chronicles contain works of various other genres: sermons,
dialogues, aphorisms, even texts of international treaties. The earliest, the *Tale
of Bygone Years* (of which there are many translations into English, most of
which render the word 'Rus'' as 'Russia'), composed in Kyiv probably in the
eleventh or early twelfth century, was incorporated into many subsequent
chronicle compilations; the Hypatian Chronicle includes it as well as the
Galician-Volynian Chronicle (thirteenth century, 1973).

Kyiv's significance steeply declined after the destruction of the city by the
Mongol army of Batu Khan in 1240. Thereafter, the residual principalities in
what today is Ukraine's west, and Vladimir-Suzdal where Muscovy would later
arise, took their separate political and cultural ways.

Afterword

'What can the poet do in the world?' – Ivan Drach puts this question several times
in a poem titled 'Hitara Pablo Nerudy' (Pablo Neruda's Guitar, Drach 1974:
15–17). He offers three answers: the poet can celebrate the presence of beauty in
the world; rebel against injustice; or become immortal by dying for an idea.

Had Drach been writing at a time less hostile to the idea of the individuality of
the Ukrainian nation than the Soviet 1970s, he might have added that the poet
can speak on behalf of a people and celebrate it; represent that people to itself
and, possibly, the world; and defend it against those who would obliterate it. In
medieval times, it was through literature – the oratory of an Ilarion, the
storytelling of the chroniclers and the verbal portraiture of saints' and monks'
lives – that Kyiv and Kyivan Rus' learned who they were. In the days of the
effusive Baroque, it was through literature that learned churchmen, multilingual
and intellectually sophisticated, expressed loyalty to their religious and cultural
heritages while participating in the European republic of letters. In the nineteenth century, when most members of the Ukrainian cultural elite had been

recruited as servitors of different empires, it was literature and the genius of Shevchenko that turned the life and language of ordinary people into the cornerstone of a new national identity. In the three decades on either side of 1900 literature alongside the other arts made that identity modern. It was literature that, in the 1960s, squeezed through a chink in the armour of Soviet authoritarianism to assert freedom of thought and of national self-expression. It was in literature, above all, that during the years following 1991 Ukrainians experimented with ways of shedding the colonial burden of centuries.

'Shedding the colonial burden': until 2014, Ukrainians applied this metaphor to the cultural and psychological transformation, which, they believed, they themselves needed collectively to undergo in order to free themselves from the reflexes of subordination and self-deprecation to which they had been habituated by the experience of authoritarianism and cultural domination by Russia. But after 2014, and all the more so after 24 February 2022, it became clear that an even more urgent task had to be addressed first: resistance against an aggressor with resurgent colonial pretensions, contemptuous of Ukraine's sovereignty and intent upon erasing Ukraine's very identity. The war is fought on many fronts: military, diplomatic, economic, informational, technological and, of course, cultural. Poets, writers and ordinary citizens whom the war has moved to express themselves in verse or literary prose have echoed Drach's answers to his question. Some have clung to their belief in the presence of beauty (and morality, and justice) in the world; many have railed against the injustice and suffering inflicted upon them and their fellow human beings; and too many have become immortal by dying for an idea.

Abbreviations

An asterisk at the end of an entry indicates that the book is available through the Diasporiana website (https://diasporiana.org.ua/)

Unless otherwise noted, names following the title are those of translators.

100Y:	Luchuk, O. & Naydan, M. M., eds. (2000). *A Hundred Years of Youth: A Bilingual Anthology of 20th Century Ukrainian Poetry.* Lviv: Litopys.
AMUD:	Zaleska Onyshkevych, L. M. L., ed. (2012). *An Anthology of Modern Ukrainian Drama.* Edmonton: CIUS Press.*
ASUP:	Honcharuk, Z., ed. (1982). *Anthology of Soviet Ukrainian Poetry.* Kyiv: Dnipro.
BLS:	Kobylianska, O. & Yaroshynska, Y. (1999). *But . . . The Lord is Silent.* R. Franko. Saskatoon: Language Lanterns.
BTS:	G. Luckyj, ed. (1986). *Before the Storm: Soviet Ukrainian Fiction of the 1920s.* Y. Tkacz. Ann Arbor, MI: Ardis.*
CIUS:	Canadian Institute of Ukrainian Studies.
EPKR:	*The Edificatory Prose of Kyivan Rus'.* (1994). W. R. Veder. Cambridge, MA: Harvard University Press for URIHU.
FCB:	Pchilka, O., Kobrynska, N., Yanovska, L., et al. (2000). *For a Crust of Bread.* R. Franko. Saskatoon: Language Lanterns.
FMU:	Bilenky, S. ed. & trans. (2013). *Fashioning Modern Ukraine: Selected Writings of Mykola Kostomarov, Volodymyr Antonovych, and Mykhailo Drahomanov.* Edmonton: CIUS Press.
FTW:	Ogan, E., ed. (1996). *From Three Worlds: New Ukrainian Writing.* Boston, MA: Zephyr.*
FUP:	Luckyj, G. S. N., ed. (1969). *Four Ukrainian Poets: Drach, Korotych, Kostenko, Symonenko.* M. Bohachevsky-Chomiak & D. S. Struk. Toronto: Quixote.*
Herstories:	Naydan, M. M, ed. (2014). *Herstories: An Anthology of New Ukrainian Women Prose Writers.* London: Glagoslav.
HKR:	*The Hagiography of Kievan [Kyivan] Rus'.* (1992). P. Hollingworth. Cambridge, MA: Harvard University Press for URIHU.
IDL:	Luchuk, O., ed. (2008). *In a Different Light: A Bilingual Anthology of Ukrainian Literature.* V. Tkacz & W. Phipps. Lviv: Sribne slovo.
IDN:	Chayka, D. & Yanovska, L. (1998). *In the Dark of the Night.* R. Franko. Saskatoon: Language Lanterns.*

List of Abbreviations 75

LU:	Ukrainka, L. (1968). *Lesya Ukrainka.* C. Bida, *Life and Work, & Selected Works.* V. Rich. Toronto: Published for the Women's Council of the Ukrainian Canadian Committee by University of Toronto Press.*
MUSS:	Luckyj, G. S. N., ed. (1995). *Modern Ukrainian Short Stories.* Rev. 1st ed. Englewood, CO: Ukrainian Academic Press.*
PBC:	Chernyavsky, M., Franko, I., Khotkevych, H. et al. (2004). *Passion's Bitter Cup.* R. Franko. N.p.: Language Lanterns.
RH:	Chernyavsky, M., Franko, I., Khotkevych, H., et al. (2004). *Riddles of the Heart.* R. Franko. N.p.: Language Lanterns.
SF:	Ukrainka, L. (1950). *Spirit of Flame.* P. Cundy. New York: Bookman.*
SRKR:	*Sermons and Rhetoric of Kievan [Kyivan] Rus'.* (1991). S. Franklin. Cambridge, MA: Harvard University Press for URIHU. *
ST:	Pchilka, O. & Kobrynska, N. (1998). *The Spirit of the Times.* R. Franko. Saskatoon: Language Lanterns.*
TIHU:	Lindheim, R. & Luckyj, G. S. N., eds. (1996). *Towards an Intellectual History of Ukraine: An Anthology of Ukrainian Thought from 1710 to 1995.* Toronto: University of Toronto Press.*
U22:	Andryczyk, M., ed. (2022). *Ukraine 22: Ukrainian Writers Respond to War.* N.p.: Penguin.
UD:	Sinchenko, O., Stus, D., Finberg, L. & Umland, A., eds. (2021). *Ukrainian Dissidents: An Anthology of Texts.* Stuttgart: Ibidem.
ULJT:	*Ukrainian Literature: A Journal of Translations.* https://tarnawsky.artsci.utoronto.ca/elul/Ukr_Lit/.
UP:	Andrusyshen, C. H. & Kirkconnell, W., eds. & trans. (1963). *The Ukrainian Poets: 1185–1962.* Toronto: Published for the Canadian Ukrainian Committee by Toronto University Press.*
URIHU:	Ukrainian Research Institute, Harvard University
WBL:	*Written in the Book of Life: Works by 19-20th Century Ukrainian Writers.* (1982). M. Skrypnik. Moscow: Progress.
WCD:	Andryczyk, M., ed. (2017). *The White Chalk of Days: The Contemporary Ukrainian Literature Series Anthology.* Boston, MA: Academic Studies Press.
WCS:	Kobylianska, O., Kobrynska, N., Yanovska, L., et al. (2000). *Warm the Children, O Sun.* R. Franko. Saskatoon: Language Lanterns.*

References

An asterisk at the end of an entry indicates that the book is available through the Diasporiana website (https://diasporiana.org.ua/)

Unless otherwise noted, names following the title are those of translators.

About the Harrowing of Hell. (1989). I. R. Makaryk. Ottawa: Dovehouse.

Amelina, V. (2022). A chomu vy skhozhi na nykh? [And Why Do You Resemble Them?] In 'Nasha krov mishalasia iz zemleiu': 10 novykh virshiv pro viinu ['Our Blood Mingled with the Soil': 10 New Poems about the War]. *PEN Ukraine*. https://pen.org.ua/nasha-krov-mishalasya-iz-zemleyu–10-novih-virshiv-pro-vijnu.

Andievska, E. (2022). *A Novel about a Good Person*. O. Rudakevych. Edmonton: CIUS Press.

Andrukhovych, S. (2024). *Felix Austria*. V. Chernetsky. Cambridge, MA: Harvard University Press for URIHU.

Andrukhovych, Y. (1998). *Recreations*. M. Pavlyshyn. Edmonton: CIUS Press.

Andrukhovych, Y. (2005). *Perverzion*. M. M. Naydan. Evanston, IL: Northwestern University Press.

Andrukhovych, Y. (2008). *The Moscoviad*. V. Chernetsky. New York: Spuyten Duyvil.

Andrukhovych, Y. (2015). *Twelve Circles*. V. Chernetsky. New York: Spuyten Duyvil.

Andrukhovych, Y. (2018a). *My Final Territory: Selected Essays*. Toronto: University of Toronto Press. Rev. ed. 2023.

Andrukhovych, Y. (2018b). *Songs for a Dead Rooster*. V. Chernetsky & O. Kin. Sandpoint, ID: Lost Horse.

Andrukhovych, Y. (2024). *Set Change*. O. Kin & J. Hennessy. New York: NYRB Poets.

Antonenko-Davydovych, B. (1980). *Behind the Curtain*. Y. Tkach [Tkacz]. Doncaster: Bayda.*

Antonenko-Davydovych, B. (1986). *Duel*. Y. Tkach [Tkacz]. Melbourne: Lastivka.

Antonych, B. I. (1977). *Square of Angels: Selected Poems*. M. Rudman, P. Nemser & B. Boychuk. Ann Arbor, MI: Ardis.*

Antonych, B.-I. [B. I.]. (2010). *Essential Poetry of Bohdan Ihor Antonych*. M. M. Naydan. Lewisburg, PA: Bucknell University Press.*

Asher, O. (1983). *Letters from the Gulag: The Life, Letters, and Poetry of Michael Dray-Khmara*. New York: R. Speller.

Babel, I. (1929). *Red Cavalry*. N. Helstein. New York: Knopf.

Bazhan, M. (2020). *Quiet Spiders of the Hidden Soul: Mykola (Nik) Bazhan's Early Experimental Poetry*. O. Rosenblum, L. Fridman & A. Knyzhnia, eds. Boston, MA: Academic Studies Press.

Berdnyk, O. (1984). *Apostle of Immortality*. Y. Tkach [Tkacz]. Toronto: Bayda.*

Bilotserkivets, N. (2021). *Eccentric Days of Hope and Sorrow*. A. Kinsella & D. Orlowsky. Sandpoint, ID: Lost Horse.

Bilotserkivets, N. (2022). *Subterranean Fire*. London: Glagoslav.

Boychuk, B. (1989). *Memories of Love*. D. Ignatow & M. Rudman. Riverdale-on-Hudson, NY: Sheep Meadow.

Burstin, E. H. (2020). On the Other Side: Dina Lipkis, Yiddish Poet of 1920s Kyiv. In *Cossacks in Jamaica, Ukraine at the Antipodes: Essays in Honor of Marko Pavlyshyn*. A. Achilli, S. Yekelchyk & D. Yesypenko, eds. Boston, MA: Academic Studies Press, pp. 439–56.

Chekh, A. (2020). *Absolute Zero*. O. Jennings & O. Lutsyshyna. London: Glagoslav.

[Chyzhevsky] Čyževs'kyj, D. (1997). *A History of Ukrainian Literature (From the 11th to the End of the 19th Century)*. 2nd ed. Englewood, CO: Ukrainian Academic Press.*

Denysenko, L. (2013). *The Sarabande of Sara's Band*. M. M. Naydan & S. Bednazh. London: Glagoslav.

Dibrova, V. (1996). *Peltse* and *Pentameron*. H. Hryn. Evanston, IL: Northwestern University Press.

Domontovych, V. (2024). *On Shaky Ground*. O. Rosenblum. N.p.: Central European University Press.

Dovzhenko, O. (1979). *The Enchanted Desna*. A. Bilenko. Kyiv: Dnipro.

Drach, I. (1974). *Korin' i krona* [Root and Crown]. Kyiv: Radians'kyi pys'mennyk.

Drach, I. (1978). *Orchard Lamps*. D. Halpern, S. Kunitz, P. Nemser et al. New York: Sheep Meadow.*

Drozd, V. (2007a). Everything All Over Again. A. Bilenko. *ULJT*, **2**, 77–85.

Drozd, V. (2007b). Fame. A. Bilenko. *ULJT*, **2**, 71–6.

Drozd, V. (2007c). The Seasons. A. Bilenko. *ULJT*, **2**, 59–70.

[Dziuba] Dzyuba, I. (1968). *Internationalism or Russification? A Study in the Soviet Nationalities Problem*. London: Weidenfeld and Nicolson.*

Finnin, R. (2022). *Blood of Others: Stalin's Crimean Atrocity and the Poetics of Solidarity*. Toronto: University of Toronto Press.

Forché, C. & Kaminsky, I., eds. (2023). *In the Hour of War: Poetry from Ukraine*. Medford, MA: Arrowsmith.

Franko, I. (1948). *Ivan Franko, the Poet of Western Ukraine*. P. Cundy. New York: Philosophical Library.*

Franko, I. (1973). *Moses and Other Poems.* V. Rich & P. Cundy. New York: Shevchenko Scientific Society.

Franko, I. (1979). *The Master's Jests.* R. Tatchyn. New York: Shevchenko Scientific Society.*

Franko, I. (1983). *Ivan Vyshensky: A Poem.* R. Tatchyn. New York: Shevchenko Scientific Society.

Franko, I. (2000). *Fox Mykyta.* B. Melnyk. Toronto: Basilian Press.*

Franko, I. (2023a). *Boryslav in Flames.* Y. Tkacz. London: Glagoslav.

Franko, I. (2023b). *Stolen Happiness.* A. Zatsepina. https://ukrdrama.ui.org.ua/en/play/stolen-happiness.

Franzos, K. E. (1883). *The Jews of Barnow.* W. M. McDowall. New York: D. Appleton. www.gutenberg.org/files/34617/34617-h/34617-h.htm.

Franzos, K. E. (1888). *For the Right.* G. Macdonald. New York: Harper & Brothers. www.gutenberg.org/ebooks/36904.

Gabor, V. (2023). *A Book of Exotic Dreams and Real Events.* P. Corness, N. Pomirko & O. Bunio. 2nd ed. N.p.: Sova.

Galician-Volynian Chronicle (1973). G. A. Perfecky. München: Fink.*

Hannover, N. (1950). *Abyss of Despair.* A. J. Mesch. New York: Bloch.

Holota, L. (2015). *Episodic Memory.* S. Komarnytskyj. N.p.: Kalyna Language.

[Honchar, O.] Gonchar, A. (1950). *Standard-Bearers: A Novel in Three Parts.* Moscow: Foreign Languages.

Honchar, O. (1989). *The Cathedral.* Y. Tkacz & L. Rudnytzky. Philadelphia, PA: St. Sophia Religious Association of Ukrainian Catholics.

Horikha Zernia, T. (2023). *Daughter.* D. Gibbons. Oakville: Mosaic Press.

[Hutsalo] Gutsalo, Y. (1974). *A Prevision of Happiness and Other Stories.* Moscow: Progress.

Ilf, I. & Petrov, E. (1932). *The Little Golden Calf.* C. Malamuth. New York: Farrar & Rinehart.

Ilf, [I.] & Petrov [Y.] (1961). *The Twelve Chairs.* J. H. C. Richardson. New York: Vintage.

Ilnytzkyj, O. S. (1997). *Ukrainian Futurism: 1914–1930: A Historical and Critical Study.* Cambridge, MA: Harvard University Press for URIHU.

Izdryk, [Y.]. (2006). *Wozzeck.* M. Pavlyshyn. Edmonton: CIUS Press.

Kalynets, I. (1990). *Crowning the Scarecrow: Appeals to Conscience in Lviv, 1968–1969.* M. Carynnyk. Toronto: Exile.*

Kalynets, I. (2014). Four Cycles of Poems. V. Hruszkewycz. *ULJT,* **4**, 157–86.

Kalytko, K. (2022). *Nobody Knows Us Here and We Don't Know Anyone.* O. Jennings & O. Lutsyshyna. Sandpoint, ID: Lost Horse.

Khersonska, L. (2023). *Today Is a Different War.* O. Livshin, A. Janco, M. Chhabra & L. Fridman. Boston, MA: Arrowsmith.

Khromeychuk, O. (2022). *The Death of a Soldier Told by His Sister.* London: Monoray.

Khvylovy, M. (1986). *The Cultural Renaissance in Ukraine: Polemical Pamphlets, 1925–1926.* M. Shkandrij. Edmonton: CIUS.*

Kiyanovska, M. (2022). *Voices of Babyn Yar.* O. Maksymchuk & M. Rosochinsky. Cambridge, MA: Harvard University Press for URIHU.

Kobylianska, O. (2000). *Nature.* L. Budna. Chernivtsi: Misto.

[Kobylianska] Kobylians'ka, O. (2001). *On Sunday Morning She Gathered Herbs.* M. Skrypnyk. Edmonton: CIUS Press.*

Kononenko, E. (2013). *A Russian Story.* P. Corness. London: Glagoslav.

Kostenko, L. (1990). *Selected Poetry: Wanderings of the Heart.* M. M. Naydan. New York: Garland.

Kostenko, L. (2002). *Landscapes of Memory.* M. M. Naydan & O. Luchuk. Lviv: Litopys.

Kotliarevsky, I. (2004). *Aeneid.* B. Melnyk. Toronto: Basilian Press. https://library.pl.ua/books/Eneida/Text_English.htm.

[Kotsiubynsky] Kotsiubinsky, M. (1958). *Chrysalis and Other Stories.* J. Guralsky. Moscow: Foreign Languages.

Kotsiubynsky, M. (1973). *The Birthday Present and Other Stories.* A. Mistetsky. Kyiv: Dnipro.

[Kotsiubynsky] Kotsiubinsky, M. (1980). *Fata Morgana and Other Stories.* Kyiv: Dnipro.

Kotsiubynsky, M. (1981). *Shadows of Forgotten Ancestors.* M. Carynnyk. Littleton, CO: Ukrainian Academic Press for the CIUS.*

Kotsiubynsky, M. (2017). *Intermezzo.* Daryna. https://medium.com/@loopyspacey/intermezzo-by-mykhailo-kotsiubynsky-translation-from-ukrainian-eb85f2cffa69.

Kraszewski, J. I. (1891). *Iermola.* M. Carey. New York: Dodd, Mead. www.gutenberg.org/ebooks/37622.

Krevza, L., & [Krevza, L., & Kopystens'kyj, Z.] (1995). *Lev Krevza's A Defense of Church Unity and Zaxarija Kopystens'kyj's Palinodia, Part I: Texts.* B. Strumiński. Cambridge, MA: Harvard University Press for URIHU.

Kruk, H. (2023). *A Crash Course in Molotov Cocktails.* A. Glaser & Y. Ilchuk. Medford, MA: Arrowsmith.

Kruk, H. (2024). *Lost in Living.* A. Kinsella & D. Orlowsky. Sandpoint, ID: Lost Horse.

Kudryavitsky, A., ed. and trans. (2017). *The Frontier: 28 Contemporary Ukrainian Poets.* London: Glagoslav.

Kulish, M. (1975). *Sonata pathétique.* G. S. N. Luckyj & M. Luckyj. Littleton, CO: Ukrainian Academic Press.

Kulish, M. (1996). *Blight*. M. Popovich-Semeniuk & J. Wordsworth. New York: LEGAS.

Kulish, P. (1973). *The Black Council*. G. S. N. Luckyj & M. Luckyj. Littleton, CO: Ukrainian Academic Press.

Kurkov, A. (2001). *Death and the Penguin*. G. Bird. London: Harvill.

Kurkov, A. (2014). *Ukrainian Diaries: Dispatches from Kiev [Kyiv]*. S. Taylor & A. Love. Darragh: Harvill Secker.

Kurkov, A. (2020). *Grey Bees*. B. Dralyuk. London: MacLehose.

Kurkov, A. (2022). *Diary of an Invasion*. London: Mountain Leopard.

Kvitka-Osnovianenko, H. (1940). *Marusia*. F. R. Livesay. New York: E.P. Dutton. https://tarnawsky.artsci.utoronto.ca/elul/Main-Eng.html.

[Lefin] Levin, M. M. (1996). *Cheshbon HaNefesh: A Guide to Self-Improvement and Character Refinement*. D. Landesman. [New York]: Feldheim.

Lutsyshyna, O. (2023). *Ivan and Phoebe*. N. Murray. Dallas, TX: Deep Vellum.

Lutsyshyna, O. (2024). *Love Life*. N. Murray. Cambridge, MA: Harvard University Press for URIHU.

Lysheha, O. (1999). *The Selected Poems of Oleh Lysheha*. O. Lysheha & J. Brasfield. Cambridge, MA: Harvard University Press for URIHU.

Lysheha, O. (2022). *Dream Bridge: Selected Poems*. V. Tkacz & W. Phipps. Sandpoint, ID: Lost Horse.

Maksymchuk, O. & Rosochinsky, M., eds. (2017). *Words for War: New Poems from Ukraine*. Boston, MA: Academic Studies Press.

Maljartschuk, T. (2024). *Forgottenness*. Z. Tompkins. New York: Liveright.

Matios, M. (2010). *Hardly Ever Otherwise*. Y. Tkacz. Melbourne: Bayda.

Matios, M. (2011). *The Russky Woman*. Y. Tkacz. *Mother Marica, the Wife of Chrystofor Columbus*. P. Onyfruk. Melbourne: Bayda.

Matios, M. (2019). *Sweet Darusya: A Tale of Two Villages*. M. M. Naydan & O. Tytarenko. New York: Spuyten Duyvil.

Musakovska, Y. (2024). *The God of Freedom*. O. Jennings & Y. Musakovska. Medford, MA: Arrowsmith.

Neborak, V. (2005). *The Flying Head and Other Poems*. M. M. Naydan. Lviv: Sribne Slovo.

Ocakli, S. (2017). *The Relations of the Crimean Khanate with the Ukrainian Cossacks, the Polish-Lithuanian Commonwealth and Muscovy during the Reign of Khan Islam Giray III (1644–1654)*. PhD diss. University of Toronto.

Osadchy, M. (1976). *Cataract*. M. Carynnyk. New York: Harcourt Brace Jovanovich.

[Pateryk] Paterik *of the Kievan [Kyivan] Caves Monastery*. (1989). M. Heppell. Cambridge, MA: Harvard University Press for URIHU.*

[Pidmohylny] Pidmohyl'nyi, V. (1972). *A Little Touch of Drama*. G. S. N. & M. Luckyj. Littleton, CO: Ukrainian Academic Press.*

Potocki, J. (1960). *The Saragossa Manuscript: A Collection of Weird Tales*. E. Abbott. New York: Orion.

Potocki, J. (1967). *The New Decameron: Further Tales from the Saragossa Manuscript*. E. Abbott. New York: Orion.

Prokhasko, T. (1999). Necropolis. M. Carynnyk & M. Horban. In *Two Lands, New Visions*. J. Kulyk Keefer & S. Pavlychko, eds. Regina: Couteau Books, pp. 99–123.

Prokhasko, T. (2007/2011). The UnSimple. U. Blacker. *ULJT*, **2**, 7–57; **3**, 57–115.

Prokhasko, T. (2018). A Summer Erased. O Rudakevych. *ULJT*, **5**, 301–4.

Prokhasko, T. (2022). Essai de déconstruction. In *Love in Defiance of Pain: Ukrainian Stories*. A Kinsella, Z. Tompkins & R. Ufberg, eds. Dallas, TX: Deep Vellum, pp. 153–68.

Rafeyenko, V. (2022). *Mondegreen: Songs about Death and Love*. M. Andryczyk. Cambridge, MA: Harvard University Press for URIHU.

Rafeyenko, V. (2023). *The Length of Days: An Urban Ballad*. S. Forrester. Cambridge, MA: Harvard University Press for URIHU.

Rozdobudko, I. (2012). *The Lost Button*. M. M. Naydan & O. Tytarenko. London: Glagoslav.

Rubchak, B. (2020). *The Selected Poetry of Bohdan Rubchak: Songs of Love, Songs of Death, Songs of the Moon*. M. M. Naydan, S. Budzhak-Jones & L. M. Naydan. London: Glagoslav.

Rylsky, M. (2017). *Selected Lyric Poetry*. M. M. Naydan. London: Glagoslav.

Sacher-Masoch, L. (1921). *Venus in Furs*. F. Savage. N.p.: Private print. www .gutenberg.org/cache/epub/6852/pg6852-images.html.

Samchuk, U. (2011). *Maria: A Chronicle of a Life*. R. Franko. Toronto: Language Lanterns.*

Schulz, B. (1963). *Street of Crocodiles*. C. Wieniewska. New York: Walker.

Schulz, B. (1979). *Sanatorium under the Sign of the Hourglass*. C. Wieniewska. New York: Penguin.

Shcherbak, I. (1989). *Chernobyl [Chornobyl]: A Documentary Story*. I. Press. Edmonton: CIUS.

Shevchenko, T. (1964). *The Poetical Works of Taras Shevchenko: The Kobzar*. C. H. Andrusyshen & W. Kirkconnell. Toronto: University of Toronto Press for the Ukrainian Canadian Committee.*

Shevchuk, V. (1989). *The Meek Shall Inherit*. V. Kholmogorova. Kyiv: Dnipro.

Shevchuk, V. (2004/2007). *Eye of the Abyss*. O. Rudakevych. *ULJT*, **1**, 10–86; **2**, 87–199.

Shevchuk, V. (2010). *Lunar Pain*. Y. Tkach [Tkacz]. Melbourne: Bayda.

Shevchuk, V. (2016). *Breath of Evil*. Y. Tkacz. Melbourne: Bayda.

Shuvalova, I. (2019). *Pray to the Empty Wells*. O. Jennings. Sandpoint, ID: Lost Horse.

Singh-Chitnis, K., ed. (2022). *Sunflowers*. N.p.: River Paw.

Skovoroda, G. [H]. (1990). *Fables and Aphorisms*. D. B. Chopyk. New York: Lang.

Skovoroda, H. (2016a). *The Complete Correspondence of Hryhory Skovoroda*. E. Adams & M. M. Naydan. London: Glagoslav.

Skovoroda, H. (2016b). *The Garden of Divine Songs and Collected Poetry*. M. M. Naydan. London: Glagoslav.

Slavutych, Y., ed. & trans. (1956). *The Muse in Prison*. Jersey City, NJ: Svoboda.*

Smotryc′kyj, M. (2005). *Rus′ Restored: Selected Writings of Meletij Smotryc′kyj*. D. Frick. Cambridge, MA: Harvard University Press for URIHU.

Somov, O. (2016). *The Witches of Kyiv and Other Gothic Tales*. S. Yakovenko. N.p.: Sova.

Stefanyk, V. (1971). *The Stone Cross*. J. Wiznuk & C. H. Andrusyshen. [Toronto: Published for the Stefanyk Centennial Committee by McClelland & Stewart].*

Stepanenko, D. (2024). *Stories from the Trenches*. Y. Tkacz. East Brunswick: Bayda.

Stiazhkina, O. (2024). *Ukraine, War, Love: A Donetsk Diary*. A. O. Fisher. Cambridge, MA: Harvard University Press for URIHU.

Struk, D. S. (1973). *A Study of Vasyl Stefanyk: The Pain at the Heart of Existence*. Littleton, CO: Ukrainian Academic Press.*

Stus, V. (1987). *Selected Poems*. J. Lassowsky. Munich: Ukrainian Free University.

Sverstiuk, I. (1976). *Clandestine Essays*. G. S. N. Luckyj. Littleton, CO: Published by the Ukrainian Academic Press for the Harvard Ukrainian Research Institute.*

Svidzinsky, V. (2017). *Evasive Shadow of Life*. B. Boychuk & B. Rubchak. Edmonton: CIUS Press.

Sydorzhevs′kyi, M., ed. (2022). *Vesna ozbroiena: Antolohiia voiennoi liryky* [*Spring under Arms: An Anthology of Wartime Lyrical Poetry*]. Kyiv: Lira-K.

Symonenko, V. (1975). *Granite Obelisks*. A. M. Freishyn-Chirovsky. Jersey City, NJ: Svoboda.*

Symonenko, V. (2017). *Silence and Thunder*. M. M. Naydan. Lviv: Piramida.

Symonenko, V. (2020). *Rose Petal Wine*. Y. Tkacz. Melbourne: Bayda.

Symonenko, V. (2022). 'To a Kurdish Brother'. V. Komarnytskyj. In Fight . . . and Overcome. *Index on Censorship*, 15 March. www.indexoncensorship .org/2022/03/fight-and-overcome/.

Tarnawsky, M. (n.d.). *Ukrainian Literature in English: An Annotated Bibliography*. https://tarnawsky.artsci.utoronto.ca/elul/English/ULE/.

Tarnawsky, Y. (1978). *Meningitis: A Work of Fiction*. New York: Fiction Collective, distributed by G. Braziller.

Tarnawsky, Y. (2007). *Like Blood in Water: Five Mininovels*. Tuscaloosa, AL: University of Alabama Press.

Teliha, O. (1977). *Boundaries of Flame*. O. Prokopiw. Baltimore, MD: Smoloskyp.

Tiutiunnyk, H. (1986). *Cool Mint: A Collection of Stories*. A. Bilenko. Kyiv: Dnipro.

Tsybulko, V. (2005). *An Eye in the Belfry*. Y. Tarnawsky. Kyiv: Dmitriy Burago.

Tulub, Z. (2015). *The Exile: A Novel about Taras Shevchenko*. A. Bilenko. London: Glagoslav.

Tychyna, P. (2000). *The Complete Early Poetry Collections of Pavlo Tychyna*. M. M. Naydan. Lviv: Litopys.

Ukrainian Dumy. Editio Minor. (1979). G. Tarnawsky & P. Kilina. Toronto: CIUS.*

Ukrainka, L. (1971). *In the Catacombs*. J. Weir. Kyiv: Mystetstvo.

Ukrainka, L. (1975). *Hope: Selected Poetry*. G. Evans. Kyiv: Dnipro.

Ukrainka, L. (2024). *Cassandra: A Dramatic Poem*. N. Murray. Cambridge, MA: Harvard University Press for URIHU.

Ulianenko, O. (2018/2021). *Stalinka*. O. Rudakevych. *ULJT*, **5**, 235–69; **6**, 157–200.

Velyčkovs′kyj, P. (1989). *The Life of Paisij Velyčkovs′kyj*. J. M. E. Featherstone. Cambridge, MA: Harvard University Press for URIHU.*

Vorobiov, M. (2020). *Mountain and Flower: Selected Poems*. M. G. Rewakowicz. Sandpoint, ID: Lost Horse.

[Vovchok, M.] Stahl, P. J. [1890]. *Maroussia: A Maid of Ukraine*. C. W. Cyr, trans. from the French. New York: Dodd, Mead. https://archive.org/details/MaroussiaAMaidOfUkraine/page/n271/mode/2up.

Vovchok, M. (1983a). *After Finishing School*. O. Kovalenko. Kyiv: Dnipro.

Vovchok, M. (1983b). *Ukrainian Folk Stories*. N. Pedan-Popil. Saskatoon: Western Producer Prairie Books.*

Vynnychenko, V. (1991a). *A New Commandment*. F. Jakovenko-Novak. Woodend: Dimitry Jakovenko.

Vynnychenko, V. (1991b). *Selected Short Stories*. T. S. Prokopov. Godeffroy, NY: Guymard.*

Vynnychenko, V. (2001). *Notes of a Pug-Nosed Mephistopheles*. T. S. Prokopov. Godeffroy, NY: Guymard.

Vynnychenko, V. (2014). The 'Moderate' One and the 'Earnest' One: A Husband's Letter to His Wife. P. J. Corness & O. Bunio. *ULJT*, **4**, 109–17.

Vynnychenko, V. (2020a). *Black Panther and Polar Bear*. Y. Tkacz. Melbourne: Bayda.

Vynnychenko, V. (2020b). *Disharmony and Other Plays*. G. Mihaychuk. Edmonton: CIUS Press.

Vynnychuk, Y. (2000). *The Windows of Time Frozen*. M. M. Naydan & A. Melnyczuk. Lviv: Klasyka.

Vynnychuk, Y. (2019). *Tango of Death*. M. M. Naydan & O. Tytarenko. New York: Spuyten Duyvil.

Vyshnia, O. (1981). *Hard Times: A Collection of Satire and Humour*. Y. Tkach [Tkacz]. Doncaster: Bayda.

Yakimchuk, L. (2021). *Apricots of Donbas*. O. Maksymchuk, M. Rosochinsky & S. Lavochkina. Sandpoint, ID: Lost Horse.

Yanovsky, Y. (1989). *The Horsemen*. S. Sinhayivsky. Kyiv: Dnipro.

Yanovsky, Y. (2018). *Bayhorod*. Y. Tkacz. Melbourne: Bayda.

Yavorivsky, V. (2016). *The Chornobyl Madonna*. Y. Tkacz. Melbounre: Bayda.

Yohansen, M. (2021). *The Journey of the Learned Doctor Leonardo and His Future Lover, the Beauteous Alceste, to the Switzerland of Slobozhanshchyna*. S. Yakovenko. N.p.: Sova.

Zabuzhko, O. (2011). *Fieldwork in Ukrainian Sex*. H. Hryn. Las Vegas, NV: Amazon Crossing.

Zabuzhko, O. (2012). *The Museum of Abandoned Secrets*. N. Shevchuk-Murray. Las Vegas, NV: Amazon Crossing.

Zabuzhko, O. (2020). *Selected Poems*. A. Melnyczuk & M. Hurder, eds. Boston, MA: Arrowsmith.

Zabuzhko, O. (2022). No Guilty People in the World: Reading Russian Literature after Bucha. U. Blacker. *Times Literary Supplement*, **6212** (22 April), 7–8.

Zemlyak, V. (1982). *The Swan Flock*. A. Bilenko. Kyiv: Dnipro.

Zemlyak, V. (1984). *Green Mills*. A. Bilenko. Kyiv: Dnipro.

Zhadan, S. (2013). *Depeche Mode*. M. Shkandrij. London: Glagoslav.

Zhadan, S. (2016). *Voroshilovgrad*. I. S. Wheeler & R. Costigan-Humes. Dallas, TX: Deep Vellum.

Zhadan, S. (2018). *Mesopotamia*. R. Costigan-Humes, V. Tkacz & W. Phipps. New Haven, CT: Yale University Press.

Zhadan, S. (2020). *A New Orthography*. J. Hennessy & O. Kin. Sandpoint, ID: Lost Horse.

Zhadan, S. (2021). *The Orphanage*. R. Costigan-Humes & I. S. Wheeler. New Haven, CT: Yale University Press.

Zhadan, S. (2023a). *How Fire Descends*. V. Tkacz & W. Phipps. New Haven, CT: Yale University Press.

Zhadan, S. (2023b). *Sky above Kharkiv: Dispatches from the Ukrainian Front*. R. Costigan-Humes & I. S. Wheeler. New Haven, CT: Yale University Press.

Cambridge Elements ☰

Soviet and Post-Soviet History

Mark Edele

University of Melbourne

Mark Edele teaches Soviet history at the University of Melbourne, where he is Hansen Professor in History. His most recent books are *Stalinism at War* (2021) and *Russia's War Against Ukraine* (2023). He is one of the convenors of the Research Initiative on Post-Soviet Space (RIPSS) at the University of Melbourne.

Rebecca Friedman

Florida International University

Rebecca Friedman is Founding Director of the Wolfsonian Public Humanities Lab and Professor of History at Florida International University in Miami. Her recent book, *Modernity, Domesticity and Temporality: Time at Home,* supported by the National Endowment for the Humanities, explores modern time and home in twentieth century Russia (2020). She is one of the editors for the Bloomsbury Academic series *A Cultural History of Time.*

About the Series

Elements in Soviet and Post-Soviet History pluralise the history of the former Soviet space. Contributions decolonise Soviet history and provincialise the former metropole: Russia. In doing so, the series provides an up-to-date history of the present of the region formerly known as the Soviet Union.

Cambridge Elements ≡

Soviet and Post-Soviet History

Elements in the Series

Printed in the United States
by Baker & Taylor Publisher Services